No One Way

Teaching and Learning
in Higher Education

Patricia Cranton

Wall & Emerson, Inc.
Toronto, Ontario ● Dayton, Ohio

Orders for this book or requests for permission to make copies of any part of this work should be sent to:

Wall & Emerson, Inc.
Six O'Connor Drive
Toronto, Ontario, Canada M4K 2K1

Telephone: (416) 467-8685
Fax: (416) 696-2460
E-mail: wall@wallbooks.com
Website: www.wallbooks.com

Canadian Cataloguing in Publication Data

Cranton, Patricia
    No one way

Includes bibliographical references and index.
ISBN 1-895131-17-0

1. College teaching.   2. Education, Higher.   I. Title.

LB2322.2.C73 1998   378.1'25   C97-931774-6

Printed in Canada.

1 2 3 4 5 6 7 8   07 06 05 04 03 02 01 00 99 98

Table of Contents

Preface   **vii**

Chapter One:

Goals of Teaching and Learning in Higher Education   **1**

Three Learning Goals in Higher Education   3

Knowing About Teaching   12

Gaining Knowledge about Teaching
     through Reflection   18

Summary   20

Chapter Two:

The Changing Context of Higher Education   **23**

The Changing Landscape in Colleges and
     Universities   25

Social and Political Influences   35

Partnerships with Business and Industry   38

Institutional Constraints   40

Summary   44

Chapter Three:

Teachers and Learners as Individuals   **47**

Psychological Type Preferences   48

Teaching Style Preferences   55

Learning Style Preferences   61

Summary   67

Chapter Four:

Planning for Teaching and Learning   **69**

Articulating a Philosophy of Practice   71

Curriculum Development   75

Preparing Learning Experiences   88

Summary   95

Chapter Five:

**Transmitting Instrumental Knowledge and
Technical Skills**   **97**

Lectures and Demonstrations   98

Problem-Based Learning   104

Experiential Learning   108

Critical Thinking   114

Summary   118

Chapter Six:

Facilitating Communicative Knowledge   121

Discussion   123

Collaborative Learning through Group
   Work   129

Role Plays and Case Studies   134

Networks and Support Groups   138

Summary   141

Chapter Seven:

Fostering Emancipatory Learning   145

Critical Self-Reflection through Journal
   Writing   147

Critical Debate and Critical Questioning   151

Articulating and Examining Assumptions   156

Summary   167

Chapter Eight:

Evaluating Learning and Teaching   169

Providing Feedback to Students   171

Giving Meaningful Evaluations   174

Student Self-Evaluation   179

Evaluating Teaching   184

Summary   189

Chapter Nine:

Teaching Excellence: Case Studies   **191**

Teaching Excellence and Teacher
  Preferences   207

Who is the Perfect Teacher?   209

References   **213**

Index   **221**

Preface

Colleges and universities across North America are placing increasing emphasis on the quality of teaching in their institutions. In Canada, the Smith Report stresses the need for improved instruction and better resources for faculty development. In the United States, a survey of more than 23,000 academics in 47 institutions found that faculty and administrators believe a higher value must be placed on teaching. As a result of this growing concern, attention is turning to how faculty acquire their teaching skills and what administrators can do to foster good teaching.

Background

The current literature for teachers in higher education falls into several categories. There are collections of guidelines and tips for classroom presentation, books on evaluating student learning, resources devoted to instructional design and curriculum development, and materials on faculty evaluation. This literature tends to focus on more traditional teaching methods and hence on only one domain of knowledge. It defines teaching as time spent in the classroom "delivering" instruction, thereby neglecting the broad array of other activities carried out by faculty in order to facilitate learning—for example, planning learning activities, meeting with students individually, counselling, working with colleagues, and keeping up with developments in the field.

Recently, specialized books have appeared on specific teaching innovations, such as collaborative learning strategies, fostering critical thinking, active learning, cooperative education and experiential learning, distance education, technology-based learning, classroom research techniques, problem-based curriculum, and professional education. As important and interesting as this literature is, it does not address the more general needs of a faculty member or graduate teaching assistant who wishes to learn more about teaching.

The current emphasis on the quality of teaching in higher education, the lack of teacher training or preparation for faculty, the undervaluing of teaching by institutional systems, and the restricted nature of the available literature combine to create a strong need for a comprehensive and theoretically grounded, yet practical, book on teaching and learning in colleges and universities.

Need

Most faculty are hired on the basis of their subject-area expertise or accomplishments as researchers rather than their teaching competence. At universities especially, it is assumed that a good researcher will also be a good teacher. New faculty are encouraged to carry out research and publish articles and books. And in most colleges, instructors are left to their own devices when it comes to learning about teaching. Although professional development programs often exist, they tend to be underfunded and understaffed; any comprehensive or systematic approach to enhancing the quality of teaching is rare. Yet faculty do care about their teaching and would like to know how to do a better job, and institutions of higher education do want their faculty to be good teachers. But the conflict between institutional philosophies that espouse excellence in teaching and actual institutional systems of hiring, rewards, recognition, and resources for professional development place most faculty in a difficult position. Where and how do they learn about teaching?

Without the opportunity to learn about teaching, faculty tend to use the same, usually traditional, methods that they experienced as students. Thus, they present information through lectures, give demonstrations of technical skills, and evaluate learning with multiple-choice tests. Such methods are indeed effective in certain disciplines and circumstances (e.g., for transmitting instrumental knowledge), but probably do not foster the higher level learning and critical thinking that are among the goals of higher education.

In this book, I address the need for an integrative, comprehensive approach to teaching and learning in higher education. Based on a philosophical framework comprised of psychological types and domains of knowledge, teaching strategies and methods are presented that not only transmit knowledge and skills, but also facilitate communicative knowledge and foster emancipatory learning.

Purpose and Audience

This book has two purposes. First, teaching and learning in higher education is placed in a comprehensive and theoretically grounded, but easily understood, framework. Second, based on this perspective, practical strategies are provided for readers who are learning about teaching.

The objectives of the book are to:
- identify the goals of higher education;
- relate these goals to current social conditions;
- view teachers and learners as individuals;
- provide strategies for planning teaching;
- present guidelines for transmitting instrumental knowledge;
- suggest ways to facilitate communicative learning;

- encourage faculty to foster emancipatory learning;
- illustrate teaching excellence through the use of case studies.

The primary audience for this book comprises both experienced and beginning college and university teachers who care about their practice. They will find practical strategies and ideas for use in the classroom, learn how strategies vary for different kinds of knowledge, and be able to identify the kinds of knowledge with which they work. In addition, the book encourages faculty to view their teaching within the larger framework of the goals and contexts of higher education.

Another audience consists of teaching assistants and seminar leaders in universities. Training programs for these individuals are already in place in many universities, ranging from short orientation sessions to workshops and courses on teaching and learning in higher education. For all of these programs this book could be used as a text.

Finally, instructional and faculty developers at colleges and universities will find the book useful for their practice.

Overview of the Contents

In the introductory chapter, the overall framework for the book is laid out in a discussion of three primary goals of higher education. Each of these goals is related to a domain of knowledge.

Colleges and universities have changed in ways that influence the nature of teaching. In Chapter Two, I discuss how altering circumstances serve to influence teaching strategies, course content, program goals, and our work with individual students.

We all have different experiences, backgrounds, values, preferences, and personalities. In our search for the best teaching strategies, we often overlook the importance of these individual differences. In Chapter Three, I use psychological type theory as a basis for considering differences in teaching style and learning style.

In Chapter 4, I provide planning techniques for three different levels of instruction: developing a philosophy of practice, curriculum development, and creating learning experiences.

Although no one field consists exclusively of one kind of knowledge, such areas as the sciences, health professions, trades, and technologies tend to stress instrumental knowledge. In Chapter Five, I offer strategies and guidelines for lectures and discussions, problem-based learning, and experiential learning. Ways to encourage critical thinking, one of the goals of higher education, are also discussed.

Interpretive or communicative knowledge is an understanding of each other, our social standards, and our culture. In Chapter Six, I examine teaching and learning methods that are likely to facilitate the acquisition of communicative knowledge.

Desire for self-knowledge and freedom from constraint is universal. In Chapter Seven, I draw on the adult education literature to present practical strategies for fostering emancipatory learning in colleges and universities.

In Chapter Eight, I turn to the evaluation of learning and teaching. Providing feedback to students, giving meaningful evaluations, and encouraging learner self-evaluation are discussed. The evaluation of teaching through the use of a teaching dossier is advocated.

Finally, in Chapter Nine, I present four case studies of teaching excellence, each from a different discipline, two from research universities and two from colleges.

Acknowledgments

I would like to acknowledge the students and colleagues with whom I have worked to further my understanding of teaching and learning in higher education.

I am grateful to Byron and Martha Wall for their comments and encouragement during the development and completion of this book.

I want to thank Robert Knoop for his unfailing support and understanding.

The Author

Patricia Cranton received her B.Ed. degree (1971) and M.Sc. degree (1973) from the University of Calgary, and her Ph.D. degree (1976) from the University of Toronto in measurement, evaluation, and computer applications.

Cranton's main research interests have been the evaluation of teaching in higher education, instructional development, self-directed learning, and transformative learning. She was selected as a Distinguished Scholar at Brock University in 1991 in recognition of her research and writing. She received the Ontario Confederation of University Faculty Association's Teaching Award in 1993 and the Lieutenant Governor's Laurel Award in 1994 for an outstanding contribution to university teaching.

Patricia Cranton's previous books include *Planning Instruction for Adult Learners* (1989), *Working with Adult Learners* (1992), *Understanding and Promoting Transformative Learning: A Guide for Educators of Adults* (1994), and *Professional Development as Transformative Learning: New Perspectives for Teachers of Adults* (1996).

From 1976 to 1986, Patricia Cranton was at McGill University in the Centre for Teaching and Learning and the Department of Educational Psychology and Counselling. From 1986 to 1996, she was at Brock University in the Faculty of Education. She founded Brock University's Instructional Development Office and directed it from 1991 to 1996. Patricia Cranton is now an independent educator and consultant.

Chapter One

Goals of Teaching and Learning in Higher Education

In colleges and universities around the world, the need for better, more effective teaching is increasingly emphasized as public sector institutions attempt to justify and retain their share of diminishing funds. Faculty face growing pressure to be more innovative, cope with larger classes, provide more individual guidance for students—in short, to do a better job of teaching with more students, fewer resources, and less support. In addition, faculty are expected to provide improved instruction despite having had little or no preparation for the role of teacher and with the knowledge that good teaching brings few tangible rewards.

Faculty do care about their teaching and their students' learning. Even though public praise for our accomplishments is rare and promotion based solely on teaching excellence is unlikely, we constantly strive to share our expertise and convey our enthusiasm to our students. Believing this—that teachers in higher education want to and can enhance their practice—I attempt, in this book, to demystify the teaching and learning processes and suggest practical strategies for working with students.

Teaching and learning are complex, passionate, exhilarating, and sometimes devastating processes. Among ourselves we are usually rather secretive about our teaching, reluctant either to share our failures with others for fear of feeling foolish, or describe our successes for fear of appearing boastful. Colleagues rarely enter our classrooms or discuss their own classroom practice. We struggle in private to discover how we could have organized a lesson more clearly, involved more students in a discussion, challenged participants to be more critical of a theory, dealt more effectively with an aggressive, opinionated group member, or criticized a student's work less harshly. In the classroom, we intuitively adjust, react, and adapt what we do to the mood and responses of students. Sometimes everything works. Other times our most brilliant plans fall flat.

Teaching is not predictable. Knowledge about teaching is not the same as knowledge about a mechanical or scientific process—there are few obvious general, objective principles that can be applied to educational practice. Rather, knowing about teaching consists of knowing how others learn, how to communicate with others, and how to organize and convey our subject matter. In addition, it includes understanding ourselves as teachers and recognizing the social norms and climate within which we work. In one area of expertise, we are specialists in our discipline, whether it is language, nursing, or philosophy. In another area, we have learned how to work with our discipline in a way that leads others to learn about it—this is the unpredictable and exhilarating world of teaching.

In this chapter, I describe the commonly accepted learning goals of higher education. In order to distinguish among the kinds of learning these goals advocate in a way that is meaningful for educational practice, I draw upon Habermas's (1971) categorization of our natural human interests and the knowledge that results from these interests. I argue, in subsequent chapters, that the methods and strategies we use to promote student learning need to correspond to the kind of knowledge we want students to obtain. Second, since it is a goal of this book to enhance knowledge about teaching, I use the same framework to differentiate how we carry out our teaching. Third, I discuss three different ways in which we reflect on our teaching experiences, thereby developing and expanding our knowledge about teaching. Being clear about what we hope students will learn, what we know about teaching, and how we obtain that knowledge are all vital aspects of our goals in higher education.

Three Learning Goals in Higher Education

Anyone who has worked on or examined the current mission statements of colleges, universities, or programs within an institution may be somewhat skeptical of their lofty aspirations. Critical thinking, autonomy, lifelong learning, and student empowerment are but a few of the goals included. When we review day-to-day activities in our own and our colleagues' classrooms, it may be hard to reconcile these ideals with the realities of practice. The students want to know what is going to be on the examination or how many pages long their papers should be. We want to know how to keep them interested and involved in the course content. Producing critical, autonomous, lifelong, empowered learners is a goal that we espouse, but one that may be beyond our immediate practical concerns or in conflict with the constraints in our practice.

However, if the goals of higher education are considered in a way that takes into account the different kinds of learning we want to promote, some of this tension between goals and practice can be resolved. I place the goals of higher education within three domains: transmitting instrumental knowledge and technical skills, facilitating communicative knowledge, and fostering emancipatory learning.

Transmitting Instrumental Knowledge and Technical Skills

People have always sought to know and understand the world around them, motivated by their natural curiosity about how things work. In order to meet their needs for food, shelter, warmth, and transportation, people have always attempted to predict and control their environment. What knowledge they did acquire through careful observation, trial and error, and the application of reason to the world around them was vital to human survival.

The belief that knowledge obtained through scientific inquiry could save humanity originated with philosophers such as Bacon and Descartes. In the early 1600s, Bacon envisioned a science which would lead to man's dominion over all the earth. He believed that science would yield inventions and techniques for the betterment of humanity, but his vision was seen as a rebellion against Christianity. Similar in some ways and writing at about the same time, Descartes proposed that every object and relation among objects could be quantified. In his view, everything could be explained mechanically.

During the Age of Enlightenment—an intellectual movement in 18th century France, Germany, and Great Britain—reason and scientific discovery replaced mysticism and superstition as our way of viewing the world. Philosophers such as Locke, Hume, and Kant led this thinking, shedding light on human affairs through rationalism.

Reason, science, and empiricism have dominated our thinking ever since. Habermas (1971) and others (Bullough and Goldstein, 1984; Hoffman, 1987) label these modes of thinking as our *technical interests* leading to *instrumental knowledge*. It is this instrumental knowledge that allows us to manipulate and control the environment, predict observable physical and social events, and take appropriate actions (Mezirow, 1981). Empirical or natural scientific methodologies produce technically useful knowledge, the knowledge necessary for industry and production in modern society.

In this paradigm, knowledge is established by reference to external reality, using the senses. There is an objective world made up of observable phenomena. The laws governing physical and social systems can be identified through science, and these systems are seen to operate independently of human perceptions (who we are as individuals does not determine the reality of the world). Descartes viewed the internal world of human beings as completely separate from the external world; this is known as "Cartesian dualism" in philosophy.

One important goal of higher education is the transmission of instrumental knowledge and technical skills. A large proportion of what we want our students to learn is knowledge of this kind. For example, in trades and technology programs at the college level or in institutes of technology, students must be given practical, concrete information in such areas as marine or automobile mechanics, silviculture, dental hygiene, or computer and electronic communications. In the health professions at universities and colleges, students learn about anatomy and medications. The curricula in the sciences are derived directly from the empirical-analytical approach, whether it be biology, chemistry, physics, or geological sciences. Similarly, mathematics, computer science, and environmental science are primarily based on instrumental knowledge. In the social sciences and the humanities, many introductory courses present the basic factual or historical material required for later understanding, information which is instrumental knowledge. Studies of quantitative methods and accounting procedures in schools of business and statistics courses in psychology, sociology and education also stress technical skills and instrumental learning.

At the higher levels of any discipline, however, knowledge becomes interpretive rather than empirical. Students working at the advanced levels of trades, technologies, and sciences, will discover uncertainties and shades of meaning that can be construed in different ways.

Habermas (1971) criticizes instrumental rationality when it becomes such a pervasive ideology that we either believe all knowledge is instrumental or try to fit all knowledge into that category. The methods of science have been imposed onto our exploration of human behavior in such areas as personality, interpersonal relations, social culture, political issues, aesthetics, and morality. In the Age of Enlightenment, the application of reason or instrumental rationality was seen as the way to solve the world's problems. As a result, empirical scientific methods of observation, hypothesis, and experimentation were viewed as superior to subjective, qualitative, or spiritual ways of knowing. Practitioners and scholars alike tried to use this superior way of thinking about their discipline, regardless of the nature of the subject matter. Only recently, has "modernism" (the reign of logic) been criticized in the social sciences and education (for example, see Giroux, 1991).

This is not to say that technical skills and instrumental knowledge are unimportant. Quite the reverse. Present post-industrial society and the communications age that lies ahead have their foundations in instrumental knowledge. The transmission of this knowledge to students is a critical and essential goal of higher education. But, we need to maintain a wider perspective which recognizes that this is not the only goal of our practice. As I discuss in Chapter Five, the transmission of instrumental knowledge relies on teaching methods that fundamentally differ from those that facilitate communicative and emancipatory learning. For this reason we need to be clear about the kind of knowledge we are working with.

Facilitating Communicative Knowledge

In addition to wanting to control our environment to meet our physical needs, people also want to understand each other. Habermas (1971) calls this a *practical interest*, leading to *communicative knowledge*. From our very beginnings, we have been social creatures, forming groups, tribes, communities, cultures, and nations in order to satisfy our mutual needs and interests. To do this, we have had to learn to understand each other and have used language to do so. Whether attempting to understand a neighbor, a friend, a spouse, the community, or the country in which we live, we strive to find common ground for communication. When our communicative knowledge is inadequate or breaks down, we argue with our friends and neighbors, divorce our spouses, leave our communities, break with our country, or go to war with another country.

Hoffman (1987, p. 235) clearly describes our practical interests and communicative knowledge: "Humanity has a practical cognitive interest, an interest in maintaining and expanding communication, because we must communicate with each other through the use of inter-subjectively understood symbols within the context of rule-governed institutions. It is practical in the sense that it clarifies the conditions for communication and interaction." In order for people to survive together in groups and societies, they must communicate with and understand each other. There are no laws governing these communications; we cannot predict what our neighbor will say in response to our comment. Communicative knowledge cannot be arrived at scientifically.

When we communicate with others, we interpret what they say in our own way. We have all had the experience of listening to several people who extract, in retrospect, quite different meanings from the conversation. Examples from our personal lives probably come to mind, and it is also easy to recognize different interpretations arising across communities, cultures, or countries. For example, in Canada, communication between French-speaking and English-speaking people is viewed differently from one part of the country to another.

This does not mean that communicative knowledge is entirely individual. All societies share and transmit social knowledge, that is, a code of commonly accepted beliefs and behavior. As a society we come to agree that "that's how things should be and are" in reference to standards and values, moral and political issues, educational and social systems, and government actions. Reached through shared interpretation and consensus, communicative knowledge becomes reified—we come to believe it is objective. Carr and Kemmis (1986) state that social reality becomes objective when members of a society "define it as such and orient themselves towards the reality so defined" (p. 84)

A second goal of higher education is to facilitate communicative knowledge. Studies in psychology, sociology, politics, education, language, literature, fine arts, and history deal with communicative, as well as instrumental knowledge. In such disciplines, we study human behavior on an individual or a social scale. Programs in child studies, early childhood education, special education, social work, nursing, occupational therapy, and hospitality are all concerned with teaching students how to work with others. Broadly speaking, the goals are to increase mutual understanding of individual needs and interests and enhance social behavior so as to meet our shared interests and needs.

In disciplines where the knowledge base is instrumental in nature, learning at higher levels (for example, see Knapper and Cropley, 1991) is usually interpretive. It is here that we encourage critical thinking so that students no longer hold simplistic, black-and-white, authority-based views. Chemists, mathematicians, and statisticians all point out that research and advanced study in their discipline is far from predictable and requires high-level thinking skills.

Most models of cognitive development describe early stages in which knowledge is perceived to be certain and absolute, and later stages in which knowledge is actively constructed by individuals (for example, see Kitchener and King, 1990). If we accept this model, then regardless of our discipline, communicative learning is necessary at more advanced levels of study. An automobile mechanic, attempting to diagnose a problem based on the customer's imitation of the knocking and ticking noises in the engine, or a statistician, attempting to interpret and label the results of a factor analysis, will agree that communicative knowledge forms a component of their subject area.

Habermas (1971) points out that a serious criticism of communicative knowledge is that it is too dependent on subjective understanding. He argues that individuals may misinterpret the world around them based on distorted assumptions about themselves or society. Carr and Kemmis (1986, p. 95) write that "Social structure, as well as being the *product* of the meanings and actions of individuals, itself *produces* particular meanings, ensures their continuing existence, and thereby limits the kind of actions that it is reasonable for individuals to perform." We want social knowledge to be objective and concrete and therefore stop questioning the systems around us, unaware of the distortions that may exist in our understanding. As important as our facilitation of communicative knowledge in higher education is our ability to encourage our students to be critical, self-aware, and questioning in their approach to learning.

Fostering Emancipatory Learning

Our institutions of higher education are generally held to be sanctuaries of free thought. Traditionally, they have been independent of the agenda or influence of business, industry, or politics, thereby allowing faculty and students to be critical of conventional wisdom and innovative in their learning, thinking, writing, and research. However, as colleges and universities move toward greater public accountability, this freedom is becoming less certain. In Chapter Two I further examine the changing context of higher education and the implications for our practice. In spite of these shifts, faculty in higher education are intent on maintaining their academic freedom. Emancipatory learning remains a central goal of most college and university programs.

By nature, people are interested in self-knowledge, growth, development, and freedom. These are our *emancipatory interests*. Gaining *emancipatory knowledge* is dependent on our abilities to be self-determining and self-reflective. Self-determination can be described as the capacity both to be aware and critical of ourselves, and of our social and cultural context. Similarly, self-reflection involves being aware and critical of our subjective perceptions of knowledge, and of the constraints of our social knowledge. Emancipatory knowledge is gained through a process of critically questioning ourselves and the social systems within which we live.

Jarvis (1992) points out the paradox inherent in emancipatory knowledge. One of our deeply held principles is that people should be free and autonomous, yet much of our learning is controled by others—we live in a society "in which a great deal of public and private space is controled by others" (p. 142). People often exercise their free will, he argues, in order to conform to their culture.

The philosophical foundation of emancipatory knowledge lies in critical theory. In this approach, instrumental and communicative knowledge are not rejected, but are seen as limiting. It is argued that if we do not question current scientific and social theories and accepted truths, we may never realize how we are constrained because of their inevitable distortions and errors. History provides many examples of such "truths." At one time people accepted as fact that the world was flat. More recently, people believed that the Aryan race was superior. Without the possibility for critical questioning of ourselves and our beliefs, such distorted and constraining knowledge can be accepted by entire cultures.

Another goal of higher education is to foster emancipatory learning. As mentioned earlier, mission statements of colleges and universities often contain references to critical thinking, lifelong learning, student empowerment, and autonomy. This is emancipatory learning, an objective of many courses, programs, and disciplines. However, it is often difficult for educators to see how to work toward this goal in their own practice. In Chapter Seven, I discuss practical strategies for fostering emancipatory learning.

In all disciplines, we want our students to become aware of themselves, their learning styles, their professional goals, and their own perspectives on what they have learned. In the trades and technologies, we want our students to question the way things are done, explore new ways of doing things, and find their own place in the field. In the sciences, we want our students to be critical of accepted theories, to experiment, and to challenge current perspectives. In the social sciences, we hope that our students see beyond the existing models, are critical of the literature, and bring their own experiences to the learning situation. In education, we encourage our students to understand themselves as teachers, question the tried-and-true ways of doing things, and to be activists in educational reform. These goals may be set aside as we impart the basic knowledge in our various fields, but educators who care about their teaching and their students agree that these are their ultimate goals.

Knowing About Teaching

Faculty who do not study education as a discipline—and most of us do not, aside from the occasional professional development activity—may not think of teaching as a separate area of scholarship. In fact, this concept is relatively new to the higher education literature. Boyer (1990) discusses the study of teaching as one of four kinds of scholarly work in which faculty engage. He delineates a scholarship of discovery as pure research, a scholarship of integration as the synthesis of knowledge across time and disciplinary boundaries, and a scholarship of practice as the application of knowledge to the problems of society. His description of a scholarship of teaching includes knowledge of effective ways to represent subjects, and ability to draw the elements of a field together in a way that provides both coherence and meaning. To recognize teaching as an area of scholarship in this way is an important beginning, but I argue that knowing about teaching is still more complex than Boyer's (1990) model suggests.

A few other writers work with the idea of scholarship in similar ways. For example, based on a sociological model, Paulsen and Feldman (1995) introduce a "scholarship action system," distinguishing between a scholarship of research and graduate training, a scholarship of teaching, a scholarship of service, and a scholarship of academic citizenship.

In this section, I use Habermas's (1971) theory of three kinds of knowledge as a basis on which to describe knowing about teaching, or the scholarship of teaching. As teachers, we work with different kinds of knowledge simultaneously. In our subject, our primary area of expertise and scholarship, we are concerned with scientific, social, aesthetic, technical, or practical knowledge. In our teaching, we are concerned with the communication of that knowledge, which can be of a different nature than the subject itself. We are interested in how others learn the content of the subject. We also reflect on and work to enhance our teaching, which again can be another kind of knowledge.

Instrumental Knowledge about Teaching

Teachers have long searched for instrumental or factual knowledge about teaching. In the first half of this century, almost all educational research consisted of the application of experimental and scientific methodologies to the understanding of teaching and learning. Competency-based education, standardized curriculum packages, standardized assessment of learning, modularized instruction, and computer-assisted instruction are some examples of the outcomes of this work. Education is viewed as an input-output process in which unskilled and unknowledgeable learners enter the system, are exposed to various techniques and resources, and leave the system having learned the content as outlined by the educator. When the process fails, when people do not learn as predicted, then it is assumed that either the learners lack the ability or the prerequisite skills for the learning, or the techniques used are faulty.

This approach is attractive, especially for those faculty who present straightforward, factual, cause-and-effect kinds of content. We want to control our teaching and learn techniques to make instruction more effective. How-

ever, there are difficulties with this approach. First, the
wider societal goals and needs that education can address, especially those of critical questioning and social
reform, are not taken into account. Second, the individual
characteristics, styles, preferences, and backgrounds of
students are not considered. Third, the personal styles,
preferences, values, and backgrounds of teachers are ignored. Fourth, the complexity and unpredictability of
human communication is not recognized. Fifth, the
changing social and organizational cultures, climates,
and social contexts cannot be addressed.

Instrumental knowledge about teaching exists in some
very specific and limited areas: e.g., how to use audio-vis-
ual equipment, how to use technology in the classroom,
how to present clear and uncluttered hand-outs, how to
use one's voice in a lecture, and so forth. While this kind
of information is important and useful, it is not sufficient,
in itself, to make for effective teaching. Many of us have
fond memories of a professor who stumbled over words,
did not make eye contact, could not write legibly on the
blackboard, and yet had a profound impact on our learning and enthusiasm for the subject. I assert that knowing
about teaching is very rarely a form of instrumental
knowledge. It is natural that we seek such knowledge, for
we are interested in predicting and controling our environment and our work. The more we come to understand
teaching and learning, however, the more we realize that
it is neither entirely under our control nor subject to
established principles. Perhaps becoming a scholar of
teaching starts with this understanding. Even when the
transmittal of instrumental knowledge is our goal in
teaching, understanding the teaching process itself is not
instrumental knowledge.

Communicative Knowledge about Teaching

Communicative knowledge about teaching is constructed by faculty engaged in practice. As such, it is never static nor free of its context. Schön (1983), among others, discusses how professionals intuitively react to events while absorbed in their work—this "reflective action" leads to the development of context-specific theories of practice. Learning about teaching results from accumulating experiences in different settings, reflecting on these experiences, talking with students and other teachers, reading about teaching, and observing the approaches and styles of others. Communicative knowledge is never definitive, but rather is always fluid and open to further interpretation.

In this approach, educational goals are not ends in themselves, but criteria for the process of education as a social activity (Carr and Kemmis, 1986). In other words, there are no terminal objectives, so that when learning has been achieved, education is over. Instead, education is an on-going, socially constructed process. Neither the goals nor the techniques used to reach them are absolute or conclusive; teachers use their professional judgment based on their experience, preferences, and knowledge of the learners and the nature of the environment within which they work.

Communicative knowledge about teaching operates on several levels. For the individual, it includes an understanding of how people learn and develop, how people interact and relate to each other in groups, how communication takes place, and how personal preferences and styles are related to the learning process. At the program or curriculum level, communicative knowledge involves recognizing program goals and origins, the rationale for curricula, the relationship between the various parts of a course or a program, and how the program relates to the world of work for which students are being prepared. On a still broader scale, communicative knowledge includes awareness of the accepted standards of the community and culture in which the institution operates, the values of the institution in which the teaching takes place, the role of education in society, and the role of government and politics in education.

When one of the goals of teaching is to develop communicative knowledge, as is often the case in the social sciences and humanities, it may be easier to see that knowledge about teaching itself is a communicative process. In these disciplines, we often use strategies such as discussions, group work, and case studies in our teaching (see Chapter Six). In this way the content and the process are congruent.

Emancipatory Knowledge about Teaching

Emancipatory knowledge about teaching is gained through recognizing and rejecting distorted or limiting points of view. For example, if a faculty member works in a department which sets very difficult and tricky final examinations to weed out students in their first year of studies, and if she accepts this practice solely because it corresponds to her own experience as a student, this concurrence will limit her options for evaluating her students. Or, if another faculty member considers that higher education is accountable primarily to the needs of business and industry, this viewpoint limits his choice of teaching strategies or course content.

The intent here is *not* to make a judgment about any one practice or view. Rather, it is to emphasize that if a teacher is not aware of options and alternatives, he or she is not free to make choices. The professor who accepts without question the system of the department, institution, or context of the teaching and learning process is not an autonomous practitioner.

Emancipatory knowledge has two levels—inner self-awareness and outer action. Increased self-awareness, obtained by questioning what we do and why we do it, can lead us to reveal limited or distorted perspectives. When freeing action is taken, based on this increased awareness, changes can be made to eliminate constraints. For example, if the professor in the earlier example began to question her acceptance of departmental evaluation practices, she might become more aware of the values she holds as a teacher. If she went on to raise this issue at departmental meetings and suggest a different policy, she could begin to change the system in which she works. Her more open perspective could lead her further to change policy in the university or the profession which her program serves.

Emancipatory knowledge about teaching takes several forms. On a personal level, it includes an awareness, through critical self-reflection, of our teaching preferences and styles, the way our personality influences our choices, and the sources of our values and beliefs about teaching. It goes beyond simply understanding our preferences and values to critically questioning and considering our own and others' ideas. When an opinion is revised and action taken, based on the new viewpoint, this becomes emancipatory learning. On a program or curricular level, emancipatory knowledge encompasses criticizing existing goals and approaches, questioning the rationale for the way things are done, collecting information from students and colleagues on alternative views, and asking why it is important to question our practice. When we modify an idea that seems to us to be invalid, based on our questioning, the new knowledge is emancipatory in that it frees us from the constraint of not knowing.

Education is a process with social consequences—we influence the thinking, values, and expectations of citizens in our society. The teacher who is involved in educational reform works with others to challenge existing systems. Emancipatory knowledge includes developing an awareness of the social and historical background of higher education systems, forming critical theories, organizing processes of enlightenment, and instituting action for change (Carr and Kemmis, 1986).

Gaining Knowledge about Teaching through Reflection

At least in part, people become knowledgeable by reflecting on and making meaning out of their experiences (Brookfield, 1987; Mezirow, 1991). Thus, critical reflection on teaching is a key component of gaining knowledge about our practice (Cranton, 1994a; 1996a). For example, if we incorporate group work into a class to which we have always lectured, and if it is clear that students enjoy and benefit from the activity, we might then consider whether group work would be appropriate in other segments of the course. Similarly, if every time we try to use group work, it simply does not work out—students talk about social events or other courses rather than the issue at hand—we might then consider how we set up the activity. Were the goals clear? Did students know what to talk about? Or, we might question whether group work is suitable at all in that context. Through these reflective processes, we gain knowledge about teaching.

We normally use the term, reflection, to mean thinking about, a rational and analytical process. However, not everyone gains knowledge in a rational and analytical fashion. Some people make meaning out of their experiences intuitively, through value judgments, or the senses and impressions evoked by the experience (discussed more fully in Chapter Three). Thus, the word, reflection, which describes the way we gain knowledge through experience, includes, as well, imagination, affect, and impression, as well as analysis.

Just as student learning and ways of knowing about teaching can differ, so can reflection or ways of making meaning out of our experiences vary. One classification system includes content, process, and premise reflection (Cranton, 1994b; Mezirow, 1991).

Content reflection is a process of considering or musing upon the nature of a problem. The instructor might ask, "What did I do in class today that seemed to spark interest?" or "What could I have said that led to such confusion on that important point?" We mull over a class or a course in our minds, analyzing what happened, imagining how it could have been different, reviewing impressions of the session, or judging the feelings evoked by the experience.

Process reflection involves paying attention to how things came to be the way they are. The teacher might ask, "How was it that I didn't notice when no one understood me?" or "How did it happen that the discussion got so far off-track?" We look at what happens to cause the problem. Do we miss cues? Are we insensitive to the atmosphere of the class? Do we get so wrapped up in the content that we forget about the students? Do we so want the learners to like us that we do not challenge their views?

Premise reflection questions whether the problem is important at all. It is an examination of the underlying assumption that the problem is meaningful in the first place. The instructor might ask herself, "Why is it important that students are interested?" or "Why does it matter that they understand that point?" Mezirow (1991, p. 111) argues that premise reflection is the process by which "our belief systems—meaning perspectives—are transformed." That is, when we question whether something is worth questioning, we are challenging our own beliefs.

When the teacher who has always believed that students need to see a certain point of view questions whether or not that matters, he is confronting the validity of his own perspective.

Reflection on the content, process, or premise of an experience can take place within each of the domains of knowledge—instrumental, communicative, and emancipatory (Cranton, 1994b). For example, an instructor asks: "What are the beliefs of my institution regarding the importance of teaching?" "How did these beliefs develop as they did?" and "Why does it matter what the beliefs are?". These questions demonstrate content, process, and premise reflection on communicative knowledge. Reflection is an important and recurring theme throughout the book and is especially emphasized in Chapter Seven.

Summary

Teaching and learning are complex, unpredictable processes with very few firm principles to guide us. In teaching, we are communicating about a subject with other people, and this communication takes place within an institutional and cultural context. Language is the medium of our work—we use "inter-subjectively understood symbols within the context of rule-governed institutions" (Hoffman, 1987, p. 235).

What do we expect students of higher education to learn? Each institution, program, and course has its own set of goals, but these goals can be categorized in a way that helps us choose teaching strategies. Using Habermas's (1971) broad philosophical framework of human interests and knowledge, three goals of higher education can be delineated.

First, it is the intent of many college and university programs to transmit instrumental knowledge and technical skills—the knowledge needed to understand and operate in the world. A great deal of learning in science programs is, for example, instrumental in nature. A second goal is to facilitate communicative knowledge—an understanding of each other and the society within which we live. Disciplines that focus on the study of human interactions have this as their primary goal. Third, we always attempt to promote self-awareness, autonomy, and a critical approach to knowledge among our students. Therefore, fostering emancipatory learning is a goal in most higher education institutions in the Western world.

The same framework of instrumental, communicative, and emancipatory knowledge can be used to describe and clarify how we know about teaching. Although 20th century research tried to uncover instrumental knowledge about teaching, it does not exist, except at a superficial level. Teaching is, by definition, communicative. Knowledge about teaching is never static and is never context-free: it has to do with understanding others and the social world of education. Knowledge about teaching can also be emancipatory when the instructor questions personal or public perspectives on practice, finds them limiting, and works to make revisions.

How do we expand what we know about teaching? Most commonly, we gain this knowledge by reviewing, thinking about, and interpreting our experiences, whether those experiences occurred in the classroom, while reading, or through discussion with colleagues. Although this kind of reflection is an analytical process, it may take different forms for various individuals. When we think about our teaching, we engage in several kinds of reflection, namely, content reflection—what happened; process reflection—how did it come to be this way; and premise reflection—why is this important. In this way we further our knowledge about teaching.

Chapter Two

The Changing Context of Higher Education

Higher education is changing. Some changes are driven by economic factors—less money, fewer jobs, more students. Change also is fueled by an exponential increase in available information, technological developments, new communication patterns, greater diversity in student populations, shifting political structures, and the expanding role of business and industry in education. Once the prerogative of the elite, higher education is now essential for the efficient functioning of modern society. Universities, which traditionally stood apart from society in order to take on the tasks of challenging and transforming our ways of thinking, are now more likely to serve and maintain that society.

Faculty members believe that it is their responsibility to question conventional knowledge and have protected their right to do so through the entrenchment of tenure and academic freedom. Yet as Jarvis (1992) argues, if educators see themselves as primarily encouraging critical reflection on society's norms, the result could be the destruction of society itself. The existence of society is predicated upon agreed-upon norms. Then again, educators who strive to socialize students or perpetuate the status quo may be accused of indoctrination or, at least, conservatism. It is not my intent to explore these issues here fully, but neither can they be completely ignored because of their impact on our practice. Political questions inevitably underlie education. As teachers, we need to consider whether we are encouraging non-reflective learning, transmitting conventional knowledge, promoting individual growth and development, challenging social norms, or providing experiences through which our students can learn on their own.

Education is a means of maintaining stable systems or questioning untenable structures. In today's changing world of higher education, as integration with other social systems increases, it becomes even more important for us to make conscious decisions regarding our goals, methods and strategies, and evaluation procedures. Jarvis (1992) describes the teaching and learning process as a moral one. In whose interest are we helping students learn and develop—their own, ours, those of the profession, the institution, business, society?

In this chapter, I examine some of the ways in which higher education is changing and how these changes affect teaching. In Chapter Four's discussion of developing a philosophy of practice, some of the key decisions to be made about how we approach teaching are explored in more detail. In this chapter, I first look at how colleges and universities are affected by changes in diversity of student populations, size of classes, and composition of faculty background and experience.

Next, I discuss social and political influences on higher education, including demands for accountability and the role of government in higher education. Third, I review the movement toward forming partnerships between colleges, universities, business, and industry. Finally, the impact of institutional constraints on practice in higher education is addressed. For each of these changing contexts of our teaching, I focus on how they matter to what we do in the classroom.

The Changing Landscape in Colleges and Universities

Most faculty work in a very different environment from the one in which they were students. For example, it is no longer the case that the mature student stands out from the crowd or that classes are homogeneous in language and race. As classes are bigger, sometimes containing several hundred students, getting to know the individuals in the course is impossible. Many more students are pragmatic, searching for job-specific training, rather than displaying interest in acquiring a general liberal education. A dramatic manifestation of this change is the phenomenal growth of community colleges and their expanding commitment to meet the diverse needs of students (for example, see Walleri and Seybert, 1993).

The changing nature of institutions of higher education affects our practice. It is not my intent to analyze or provide data on how organizations have evolved (for example, see Leslie and Brinkman, 1988; Berquist, 1992), but rather to discuss how teaching in higher education has and will continue to change in response. To this end, I have selected four aspects of the college and university environment that affect us all: the growing number of mature students, greater diversity in language and culture among our students, larger classes, and the aging faculty population.

Mature Students

As people change careers more often or lose their jobs and cannot find new positions, they often return for more schooling, leading to increasing numbers of mature students in university and college classrooms. Some older students, with university degrees, take college programs hoping to obtain marketable skills; some continue on to advanced degrees while waiting for an opening in their chosen profession; some enter higher education for the first time after having been in the workforce for several years; many women return to school for financial reasons.

Whatever their motives, mature students are a growing presence on our campuses, and faculty are often uncertain as to whether or how they should change their teaching practice to accommodate them. Usually, the groups we work with are not composed entirely of mature students, except perhaps in graduate programs in the professions. The most common class composition is one in which the majority of the students are in their late teens or early twenties, as is traditional, along with a smaller proportion of older learners.

Despite the influx of mature learners, faculty rarely turn to the adult education literature for help, as they do not see themselves working primarily with adults. Brookfield (1990, p. xv) is "puzzled by the distinction some academics draw between higher education and adult education" and sees "college teaching as the teaching of people who are partially or fully immersed in the experience of adulthood." Here, and indeed throughout this book, I draw on adult education literature, which emphasizes that since all learners can be placed on a developmental continuum, there is no one exact time or place when someone is mature, or an adult. The older students in our classes are not a foreign species.

Knox (1986, p. 29) writes, "As people grow older, they become both more similar and more different. They become more similar in that they confront more and more of the widespread dilemmas of society and in that their essential self becomes more apparent. They become more different in that their specialized circumstances, abilities, and experiences produce among all adults an increasing range of individual differences within each increasing age cohort." In other words, the more mature students in our classes are as different from each other as they are from the younger students. We cannot say, "Thirty percent of my class are mature students, therefore I should use a certain technique or procedure." An examination of the more practically oriented adult education literature would be helpful for faculty (for example, Knox, 1986; Brookfield, 1990; Cranton, 1992; Heimlich and Norland, 1994). Here, I highlight some selected issues for consideration.

Cognitive Development

The classic literature on adult development tells us that people tend to evolve cognitively from unquestioning conformity to authority and a tendency to think in black-and-white terms to an awareness of varying viewpoints and an acceptance of ambiguity (Loevinger, 1976; Perry, 1970). This pattern is still accepted in current work on adult development (King and Kitchener, 1994), although there is some question as to whether the patterns of female growth are different (Belenky, Clinchy, Goldberger, and Tarule, 1986). Knox (1986) points out that the way we develop cognitively influences our preferred learning styles. For example, younger people may prefer structure and routine in order to learn; older people may tend to be more analytical or inferential in their attempts to understand.

Generally, the more mature abilities of the cognitive development continuum are those that we encourage in our students. We want them to move on from unquestioning acceptance of authority, become more aware of different perspectives, grasp complexity, be more analytical. In a class that contains more mature learners, their abilities and styles can provide a model for younger learners. Confident mature students can lead discussions and group work, and assist others in the class with the more complex and integrative activities.

Experience

The more mature an individual is, the more experience he or she has had in the world of work, the more personal growth has presumably occurred, and the more learning has taken place. Rather than worrying about how to cope with older learners, we can draw on examples and illustrations from their experience and encourage them to be models for younger learners. Incorporating the experiences of adult learners into the teaching process has long been advocated in the adult education literature (Knowles, 1980).

Confidence and Self-esteem

Although we might expect more mature learners to display the confidence that we assume comes with age and experience, this is not always the case. As Brookfield (1990), among others, points out, college and university students who have returned to school as adults may well have experienced earlier failure as learners. They may believe that they have inadequate study or writing skills, that they have been out of school too long to do as well as their younger colleagues, or even that they are not intelligent enough to learn. As faculty, we need to recognize such insecurities, be supportive, and arrange for successful learning experiences for these individuals.

Mature students also may be reluctant to change or question their familiar beliefs, habits, or routines. Brundage and MacKeracher (1980) point out that when adults find themselves in new situations, they may revert to childlike behaviors and dependencies. Brookfield (1990) argues, "Perhaps the single greatest cause of resistance to learning is fear of the unknown," and agrees with Brundage and MacKeracher by stating, "As people witness events that seem to contradict their beliefs and values, they often seem to become even more committed to them" (p. 150). It is important for faculty to have realistic expectations of all students, including more mature individuals, and to be empathic when fear and resistance to change surface. It is equally important that we do not automatically expect all mature learners to be frightened and insecure—Knox's (1986) point that people become both more similar and more different as they grow older is relevant here.

Language and Culture

Modern North America is a pluralistic society with a diverse population. Increased immigration, the influx of political refugees, and social mobility have changed the face of our college and university classrooms. When faculty enter classes in which some or many of the students come from different cultures, they face difficult and important questions—for example, how best to work with students who are learning in a second language, how to learn about the unfamiliar values or customs of their students, when to help individuals preserve their cultural values, and when to help them integrate into the new society.

Working with students who are learning in a second language poses its own special problems, but, generally, in higher education we do not see ourselves as teaching language skills unless this is our field. We expect that reading and writing proficiency are prerequisites to college and university entrance. Although some argue that reading and writing should be learned within the context of a discipline, we usually refer students in need of help to special reading or writing programs. Most institutions offer these services through counseling centers, student development offices, or courses in language studies departments. Referrals to outside help do not completely free faculty members of responsibility, however. We need to give careful feedback and constructive comments on second-language students' speaking and writing, be supportive and understanding of the difficulties of working in another language, and try to separate mastery of the subject from language skills, especially when it comes to evaluation.

Working with students from varied cultural backgrounds can be difficult, regardless of the good intentions we may have. Jarvis (1992) describes how we first internalize our culture as we are growing up, then externalize or habituate the norms and values of our culture, and finally legitimatize the resulting actions, beliefs, and behaviors. In other words, our own familiar social processes become the only right or correct way of doing things. Religious, political, and institutional practices are real, concrete, and right. Language, and therefore education as well, play important roles in our development and acceptance of culture. Jarvis (1992, p. 32) writes, "People learn the objectified language of their culture and even learn to believe that it is value free, and they learn to conform to a wide range of beliefs and practices as if they are objective."

When we work with students from cultures different from our own, it is important to remember that both we and our students believe that the way we do things is the right way of doing things. Faculty who are unaware of the integral nature of cultural values and practices may not easily see or understand the perspectives held by their students. Such behaviors as working in groups, making eye contact with the instructor, posing direct questions, interrupting others, using familiar forms of address, or meeting individually with the teacher may be unfamiliar to a student from another culture or even regarded as wrong or immoral.

We may expect students to adapt or accept and integrate into our culture, since they have chosen to study in our institution. This may be much more difficult than either we or the students expect. Brookfield (1990, p. 153) describes the "danger of committing cultural suicide." He points out that "if students are asked to contemplate too much that is new or to change in ways the culture sees as too radical, then they will be given the message that further participation calls into question their allegiance to the culture and will be dealt with summarily" (p. 153).

In addition to being supportive and referring students to helpful groups, such as an international students' club, faculty may need to familiarize themselves with the process and difficulties of cultural transition. Many institutions have an office for international students, or advisors for individuals from different cultures—people with a good understanding of the devastating experience of learning in an unfamiliar culture. Materials, workshops, and individual advice may be available to faculty, as well as students, from such a source. Students studying in a foreign culture are sometimes sponsored by international organizations, for example, the Canadian International Development Association (CIDA), or by their home governments. These sponsoring agencies or foreign embassies may have advisors who are more than willing to give guidance to faculty.

Preparing Students for the Workforce

Gone are the days when a general arts degree led to a good position, and students in higher education were not concerned about getting a job. The atmosphere that many faculty will remember from their own student days no longer exists. Students are now deeply concerned about being adequately prepared for the workforce. Dropping out of a general university program and enroling in a more job-oriented college program is not uncommon today. This shift in student expectations has several implications for our teaching.

As only a small proportion of graduating students now get jobs or gain entry to professional programs which may lead to employment, competition among students is keen. For example, if the acceptance rate into a teacher preparation program is about 4%, and if about 25% of those who complete the program actually acquire teaching positions, students will go to great lengths to be among the select few. Grades become critical. Students may take no chances exploring ideas or expressing controversial opinions, but will want to know exactly what they need to do to achieve the highest grade possible. This can be disconcerting for the educator who is interested in encouraging students to challenge assumptions and engage in critical thinking. It is equally disconcerting to work with groups of learners many of whom you know will not be able to meet their career goals.

In preparation for job hunting, students understandably want to acquire as many practical and relevant experiences as possible. The professor who has dedicated his or her life to the theoretical study of biology may not understand students' impatience with theory and their interest only in practical application. In higher education, especially in universities, we expect to find a love of learning for its own sake—a passionate involvement in the discipline. The new market-driven climate leaves less room for this approach. Faculty need to appreciate the kinds of learning experiences students are looking for and to build them into their practice.

Information and access to information through technology is expanding at an unprecedented pace. Students who are preparing for the future see this as a critical component of their education. Many of our students have grown up in the technological era and are more comfortable with it as a part of their lives than we are. Computer technology is not just one more convenient tool—there are good arguments that computers are changing how we solve problems, communicate, and remember information (Saddy, 1996). Faculty who are helping students prepare for the workforce need to be familiar with, for example, the Internet, and to provide opportunities for students to access information through the use of technology.

In our fast-changing world, people are also changing careers in a way that they have never done before. As a part of preparing students for the workforce, we are also responsible for fostering lifelong learning. We obviously cannot give students the knowledge and skills that will last for the duration of their careers. For example, many forms of knowledge and technical skills are short-lived. However, Knapper and Cropley (1991), among others, remind us students will continue to use learning abilities gained through study long after graduation. We need to help students learn how to learn, a very different process than, for example, teaching chemistry. As I mention in Chapter One and Chapter Six, learning how to learn is acquiring communicative knowledge and compels us to use different teaching strategies.

Class Size

One of the most common faculty complaints in recent years is the increasing size of classes. Growing numbers of students, spiraling costs, and diminishing budgets have led most institutions of higher education to raise the enrolments in courses. Although some argue that class size does not have a negative effect on student learning (Gilbert, 1995), this institutional change is the one with which most of us have difficulties. Centra (1993) discusses survey results in which 60% of faculty at a major research university believe that the size of the class would bias student ratings of instruction.Research on student evaluation does consistently show a small negative effect of class size on ratings when classes are over 40 in number and less than 100 (for example, see Cranton and Smith,

1986; Marsh, 1987). For very laıge classes, this effect is not found.

Since such relationships are complex—they tend to vary across disciplines and levels of instruction—it is perhaps more enlightening to consider research, such as that of Murray, Ruston, and Paunonen (1990), that demonstrates that different teachers may be better suited to teaching different sizes of classes. Faculty who receive high ratings in one type of course tend to receive lower ratings in a different type of course. Personality type, especially extraversion, appears to be related to effectiveness in type of course and size of class. This possibility is discussed further in Chapter Three.

If an instructor is facilitating communicative or emancipatory learning or teaching complex psychomotor or technical skills, the size of the class does matter. Holding discussions in large groups inevitably leaves out some students. Managing small group activities in a large class is not easy. Opportunities for students to meet individually with teachers or to get to know them are not always available with big groups. Evaluation of student learning, unless computer-scored instruments are used, can become a tremendous burden for the instructor who cares about giving quality feedback to people in the class.

Older Faculty

Decreased funding for colleges and universities has led to limited numbers of new positions, increased use of part-time faculty, larger classes, and even program cuts (for example, see CAUT Bulletin, 1995). Faculty tend not to leave a secure position if they have one; new Ph.D. graduates do not usually go straight into tenure-track positions. This trend, along with the general aging of the population, has led to the phenomenon sometimes referred to as the "greying professorate." Faculty are getting older.

The influence of the shift in age of faculty on the teaching and learning process, or even on the culture of the institution, is not clear, nor easy to evaluate. It is likely, however, that experienced faculty have a different perspective on teaching. Research on award-winning teachers shows that they have "a conceptually richer and more flexible approach to teaching and its evaluation" (Dunkin and Precians, 1992, p. 501). There is evidence that higher education faculty change their assumptions about teaching over time (Amundsen, Gryspeerdt, and Moxness, 1995). It may be that an older and more experienced faculty leads to a richer learning environment. This is supported by evidence that faculty are increasingly experimenting with teaching innovations (see, for example, Rehner, 1994; Rogers, 1992).

On the other hand, it is obvious that our perspectives on teaching and learning are formed by our experiences. Older faculty developed their views and practices at a time when the professorial role was that of the teaching scholar. Thus, the "greying professorate" may be entrenched in their view of students and scholarship, one that no longer fits so well with the changing higher education scene. They may feel insecure and frightened about new expectations of faculty and prefer that things stay the same rather than take up the challenge to innovate. Award-winning teachers and those involved in instructional development projects—the participants in the research studies cited earlier—may not represent the general faculty population.

Social and Political Influences

The changing nature of colleges and universities is often attributed to the effects of financial constraints.

Government intervention in the quality of higher education through policies that control funding has aroused
protest among most North American faculty. However,
the dramatic decreases in higher education funding are
also a product of a changing society. Colleges and universities are not isolated from the societies in which they
exist, even though institutional autonomy is a tradition
(Jones, 1994). The university today, constantly influenced
by outside forces, is no longer an "ivory tower."

I select for review three social and political issues now
having an impact on higher education and examine their
implications for teaching and learning. I draw in part on
Skolnik's (1995) report of a discussion paper released in
Ontario (OCUFA, 1994), keeping in mind that concerns
often differ in private and denominational institutions
around the world. For example, in the United Kingdom,
higher education is being called upon to serve the country
more effectively through closer links with industry and
commerce (Maclure, 1988). British government intervention is seen to have crippled academic freedom (Russell,
1993). In Australia, the government supports a funding
arrangement that responds to goals shared by the government and the institutions and includes measurement of
output, quality, and performance (Dawkins, 1988).

Publicly funded colleges and universities are now under
pressure to serve public policy objectives. This pressure
directly conflicts with our tradition of a higher educational system that is independent of outside control. Universities and colleges cannot be both instruments of
government and institutions that promote critical thinking and question social beliefs. Faculty autonomy in setting curriculum, expressing unpopular views, and
working with students to foster emancipatory learning is
being threatened. This development directly influences
teaching practice.

Public demand for accountability in universities and colleges is increasing. These demands often take the form of encouraging more direct and appropriate training of students for the workplace. To serve such public policy objectives has clear implications for teaching. Accountability involves placing a much greater emphasis on teaching and what it achieves. What this means is that colleges and universities are expected to admit more students, faculty are encouraged to emphasize teaching over research, the quality of teaching is to be improved, and our institutions are expected to serve more students from non-traditional backgrounds (e.g., mature students and minority groups). Being expected to do these things with less funding leads to some odd innovations, such as scheduling self-directed learning into the timetable (Grabove, 1996). Although most of us welcome greater emphasis on teaching, wish to improve teaching quality, and are glad that it is being recognized as an important part of higher education, the expectation that we teach more students, reduce research time, and increase the diversity of our student body leads to frustration and anxiety.

The way that funds are allocated within an institution is a powerful political tool that may produce fundamental change. As Brookfield (1990) points out, "when a large grant is awarded by a foundation or corporation to a college or university, the scramble by departments and individuals to obtain pieces of this sometimes makes Machiavelli seem fainthearted and overly scrupulous" (p. 178). Concerns about the importance of various programs or the quality of education in specific areas are quickly forgotten. When governments become responsible for the allocation of funds within institutions through a "purchase of service concept" (Skolnik, 1995, p. 10), financial support for programs and hence the existence of particular kinds of programs depends on current societal approval. Again, faculty autonomy in developing the goals and content of their practice may be diminished.

Social and political processes inevitably work their way through the system to affect the classroom. As a result of new economic trends and fundamental changes in society's view of higher education, our role is shifting from that of autonomous teaching scholar to service provider.

Partnerships with Business and Industry

Colleges and universities are responding to sharp declines in funding in a variety of ways—searching for private and corporate donations, marketing staff expertise and program innovations, seeking research contracts, and attempting to attract larger numbers of part-time students. Among these strategies is a move to foster partnerships with business and industry, a matter which has long been debated in higher education. In 1918, Veblen ([1918] 1967) argued that the governing boards of American universities had been taken over by business. He believed that this would lead to the encroachment of business principles into the academic community, thereby subverting the purpose of higher education. The same kinds of concerns are expressed by academics today—the worry that the "freedom essential to learning and inquiry" (Bruneau, 1995, p. 3) will be compromised.

Partnerships between higher educational institutions and business and industry usually involve the provision of funding to carry out applied and industry-specific research projects. The number of such agreements is growing rapidly, with Weston already reporting in 1991 a total of 175 university-related research parks in the world. Higher education needs money. In exchange for this money, industry expects access to students, faculty, and resources. Hence collaborative research meeting the needs of the industry is conducted.

How does this trend influence our teaching and learning practice? First, it changes our perspective on the purpose of higher education. When we serve business or industry, we are to some extent creating and teaching knowledge that is useful to our sponsors. This is fundamentally different from our traditional goals of asking "awkward questions about why things are the way they are, whose interests these arrangements serve, and how things might be different" (Brookfield, 1990). When the purpose of our practice shifts, the dynamics of the classroom are altered accordingly.

Programs or institutions which develop partnerships with corporations pass on some of the responsibility for determining the quality of education from the institution to the partners.

Industry typically relies on a model of quality assessment that is incongruous with the goals of higher education—the criterion is efficiency as defined through measurable performance. When we are working with communicative or emancipatory learning (see Chapter One), technical assessments are simply not valid and could force faculty to change their approach in order to meet new standards for quality or lead to troublesome evaluations.

Russell (1993), who is deeply disturbed by the changes in Britain, believes the relationship between educators and students is undermined. He argues that small classes or tutorials and seminars, where controversial ideas are most likely to be discussed, are too costly to be efficient under this system and fears that industry-financed education will lead to an emphasis on the mechanical acquisition of rote learning.

Institutional Constraints

The changing nature of higher education has led institutions to respond in a variety of ways, many of which are seen by faculty to be constraints on their teaching practice. Financial cutbacks have resulted in larger classes, fewer resources, hiring freezes, less support for professional development, more part-time instructors, giving teaching assistants more responsibility, and an increased use of distance education programs. The increasing diversity in the student population has led colleges and universities to emphasize their second language programs, counseling services, and part-time programs for mature students. Faculty often find themselves working with non-traditional student groups without having the relevant knowledge and skills for doing so. Demands for public accountability have put faculty work in the spotlight, something to which they are not accustomed and may view as an infringement on their academic freedom. The new emphasis on meeting the needs of business and industry, and training students for the workforce may also often be perceived as an institutionally imposed constraint. Several of these issues are discussed throughout this chapter. Here I focus on three institutional constraints not yet mentioned, with the understanding that each constraint is a product of other, deeper influences. I discuss limited resources, diminished support for professional development activities, and accountability and evaluation.

Resources

We have all felt the impact of changes in the availability and nature of teaching resources. Photocopying is restricted, library book orders are curtailed, and only rarely does a department or library subscribe to a new journal. At the same time, money for new technologies can often be found. For many faculty, this is puzzling and frustrating. We believe that our practice is undervalued—justification of our course needs will not produce funds that no longer exist.

There is no easy solution to this institutional constraint. Asking students to pay for photocopying of a reading collection or buy an additional text is feasible only up to a point. Our students are also often stretched financially, and if they are taking several courses, the burden can become overwhelming. We need to be as creative and innovative as possible in the face of these changing circumstances.

In some disciplines, activities, exercises, or group tasks which depend on alternative resources can be designed. For example, students can interview experts, go to a field site, conduct an experiment themselves, or implement a practical project. Using such strategies to work around a lack of printed materials offers the added benefit of increasing both student involvement and experiential learning. More such strategies are discussed in Chapters Five, Six, and Seven.

Perhaps use of the Internet is our best innovative solution to the problem of limited resources. Most colleges and universities now have, at least, the potential for student access to the Internet, and if not, this will probably soon be available. What previously were fairly primitive sources of information on the Internet have become increasingly sophisticated. Using hypertext, students can easily link from one node of information to another on the World Wide Web. Sound, graphics, and text are combined to create engaging and provocative information displays. Incorporating Internet resources into a course curriculum has the added advantage of giving students the opportunity to increase their technological skills.

Diminished Support for Professional Development

Despite calls for increased emphasis on the quality of teaching in colleges and universities, the support for faculty development has not increased. Most institutions have very small centers or units responsible for teaching development, often with part-time cross-appointed staff and limited budgets. Not surprisingly, the faculty participation rate also tends to be modest.

Support for attending conferences related to teaching in one's discipline has also become almost non-existent. What limited funds are available tend to be used to finance the presentation of research papers at conferences—in line with the belief that research is more important than teaching and that better researchers make better teachers.

Although we must continue to protest the discrepancy between calls to improve quality of teaching and the limited funding offered to do so, we must also devise ways to assist faculty in their efforts to improve their teaching. Elsewhere I have described several cost-free professional development strategies (Cranton, 1994a; 1996a). Among them are working with a colleague to observe and comment on each other's teaching, setting up discussion groups related to teaching, seeking an experienced senior faculty member to be a mentor or model, and conducting research on one's own teaching (called action research by Zuber-Skerritt, 1992). Such strategies also encourage us to be responsible and self-directed in our learning about teaching, rather than relying solely on the expertise of others.

Accountability and Evaluation

Most professionals are regularly accountable to an organization or a professional association for the quality of their practice. Performance appraisals and reviews are a normal, if not enthusiastically greeted, part of work life. Higher education faculty, however, have been mostly free of this, especially in relation to their teaching. The existence of tenure and academic freedom have been used as a defence against faculty evaluation, although that is certainly not their intent. But now, faculty are being called on to be accountable and demonstrate their competence. Many view this as a constraint on their practice.

Teaching is difficult to evaluate—it is a complex phenomenon in which many factors interact to lead to student learning and development. Student ratings of teaching are the most well-researched and commonly used form of evaluation (Centra, 1993). They measure only one facet of the process, student satisfaction, and are usually quantitative in format, a limitation for faculty working in communicative and emancipatory domains of learning. The outcome of teaching, student learning, is hard to relate directly to the quality of teaching because of the nature of the process. Knowledge of teaching and learning is communicative (see Chapter One). We cannot say that teaching causes learning in the way that we say watering plants makes them grow. Faculty who criticize the evaluation procedures used by most institutions have some valid points to make.

There are good strategies for achieving accountability that circumvent the limiting constraints of mandatory evaluation. Faculty can develop teaching portfolios or dossiers containing their own choice of materials that describe their teaching. Course outlines, letters from students, descriptions of professional development activities, and a philosophy of practice are but some of the items that can be included, along with the traditional student questionnaire results (see Chapter Eight). Classroom research (Cross, 1990) or action research, as mentioned in the previous section, provides a rich and meaningful way of understanding one's teaching and how students are learning. Working with colleagues as mentors or consultants makes teaching more public. Such strategies not only make faculty more accountable for the quality of their practice, but are also likely to enhance that quality.

Summary

We teach in a context. We work within a program or department which is a part of an institution; that institution is, in turn, a part of a community, country, political system, and a culture. The decisions that we make about our teaching need to be conscious and consciously related to the context within which we work. And that context of higher education is changing at a far more rapid pace than it has ever done before.

A walk through a campus or a visit to a classroom quickly reveals some of these changes. We see far more mature students, as people change careers and return to school. Faculty can be challenged by the different characteristics of older learners—their cognitive development, experience, and self-confidence. More students from different cultures attend most of our campuses today. This may mean that faculty are working with learners who are using their second language and who have quite different cultural norms from our own. Now many students expect and demand that their education prepare them for the workforce. For faculty absorbed by the intrinsic merit of their discipline, this can be a jolt.

Class size is continuing to grow. Some lecture halls now seat several hundred or even a thousand students; the number of students attending seminars and tutorials gradually creeps up. Our walk across campus will likely reveal crowded rooms and all rooms in use. Faculty need to adjust their strategies and come up with innovative ways of working with larger classes. Finally, we see older faculty in higher education. This means that more faculty experience and wisdom is available to students and colleagues, but this may be accompanied by less willingness to change with the changing times.

Social and political upheaveal and influence has led to a revised vision of what colleges and universities are and do. Pressure is growing to serve public policy objectives; demands for public accountability are increasing; and the allocation of funds is shifting. Each of these changes has a potentially profound impact on our practice.

Many colleges and universities are responding to decreases in funding by establishing partnerships with business and industry. Some faculty see this as an innovative solution to a difficult problem, while others believe it will result in a stifling of academic freedom.

As institutions respond to change, faculty fear that many of these changes act as constraints on their practice. There are fewer resources, less support for professional development activities, and more demands for accountability. However, faculty can respond to such perceived constraints in creative ways, simultaneously enhancing their practice.

Chapter Three

Teachers and Learners as Individuals

We all know that people learn differently. For example, I know someone who can read a textbook while listening to loud music. I have students who read books in parts—a section at the end, a section in the middle, and then back to the end. I also know people who write papers that way. However, in our teaching we either tend to act as though everyone learns the same way we do or use a variety of methods, hoping that some of them are effective with some of the students some of the time. A variation of this approach is "teaching to the middle," a spot which few students occupy.

Similarly, we know that people have different preferences in how they teach. A walk through the hallways of a college building reveals both closed and open classroom doors. Passing the open doors, we see people lecturing to both large and small groups, noisy discussions, boisterous group work, quiet laboratories, and hushed conversations. We often teach in the way that we like to be taught. If we like to listen to lectures, we may choose to give lectures; if we prefer collaborative work, we may form learning groups. Or we may teach in the way we were taught in the past, using our favourite professors as models, but still relying on our own learning preferences as a yardstick for what is good teaching. Our specific discipline and the type of knowledge we are working with may also influence teaching style (see Chapter One). Institutional restrictions can also play a role in determining what we do in the classroom, especially such constraints as large class sizes or minimal resources for teaching (see Chapter Two).

Easy answers do not exist; there are no black and white conclusions to be drawn, nor cause and effect equations in teaching and learning. What may be valid in one context with one group of people may not be so in another. No set of maxims can guarantee the correct choice of a technique or strategy. It is even difficult to find a set of generalizable principles that will lead to more effective teaching. This does not mean that what we do in the classroom is haphazard or chaotic, without rhyme or reason. We need to know about teaching and learning, come to understand ourselves as educators, then relate these understandings to our discipline and context, and thereby develop our own practice. Each educator needs to work out his or her own informed philosophy of practice.

In this chapter, I use Jung's ([1921] 1971) psychological type theory as one way of understanding individual differences. Jung's work is based on a constructivist philosophy. In other words, he acknowledges that all people make meaning of the world in their own way and that understanding each other is a subjective process. I discuss preferences for different teaching styles, using psychological type as a framework. Finally, I review individuals' preferences for learning styles in a similar fashion. The goal of this chapter is to increase understanding of how people differ from each other and to encourage the use of a variety of teaching strategies.

Psychological Type Preferences

Jung ([1921] 1971) observed patterns in the differences among people. Although he always respected the uniqueness and complexity of the individual, over time he grew to believe that these patterns were meaningful and helpful in understanding others. Jung never tried to quantify the patterns; in fact, he postulated that this might not be possible at all. Since that time, several instruments to assess psychological type have been developed and widely used (for example, see Myers, 1985). In the most recent of these, a colleague and I attempt to follow the original theory as closely as possible by including a quantitative, an interpretive, and a critical component to the assessment process (Cranton and Knoop, 1995). It is important to keep in mind that people should not be labeled as types unless they have been included in the discussion. Understanding each other is communicative knowledge.

Attitudes

All individuals have attitudes or ways of relating to the world around them. Jung suggests a continuum ranging from introversion to extraversion to explain these attitudes. Introversion is a preference for the self or the inner world; extraversion is a preference for the external world. All people are interested in both the inner and the external world, but may favor one over the other to varying degrees.

The introverted attitude leads to personalization or subjectification of experiences and events. For example, if I see that it is raining, that observation stimulates me to think about how I personally am affected by rain—that it makes me feel cozy and sleepy, or that it puts me in a bad mood. The interest is in the self, so events from the outside world set off thoughts or feelings about the self. A person who is more introverted than extraverted may appear to be withdrawn or shy to an observer—this is our common understanding of the term introverted.

The extraverted attitude is demonstrated by an interest in things outside the self. A person who is more extraverted sees the same rainy day, but may remark that there has been more rain this year than last year or that the farmers needed this rain. The interest is focused on the external world and is not internalized. A person who is more extraverted than introverted may appear to be out-going, talkative, or boisterous to an observer.

It is extremely rare for a person to be completely introverted or extraverted. Most of us display both attitudes. We may be more extraverted at work than at home, or we may have periods in our lives when we are focused more inwardly than at other times. Generally, though, we have a preference for one attitude over the other. With a tendency toward introversion, I may need to recover from a workshop or a conference by spending time by myself, with my self. Another person with a preference for extraversion might feel uncomfortable with too much quiet time and call friends on the telephone or make plans to go out.

Functions

People's attitudes do not exist in isolation but are displayed in all aspects of living. We have introverted or extraverted attitudes toward things we detect with our senses (e.g., a sunset), toward visions of the future (e.g., what will my job be like next year), toward rational judgments (e.g., a logical problem to be solved), and toward value judgments (e.g., the importance of family). Jung ([1921] 1971) described these as the four functions of living. He observed that people tend to have preferences as to which functions they like to use.

There are two *judgmental* functions—two opposing ways of making judgments. A person can use a logical, analytical process of *thinking* or a subjective, valuing process called *feeling*. If I were to make a judgment about a change in job responsibilities using my thinking function, I might list the advantages and disadvantages of taking on the new responsibilities. I might read any documentation available or ask others for information. Then I would logically make my judgment. If you were to make the same judgment, using your feeling function, you might rely on a deep-seated, value-based reaction of acceptance or rejection. You might consider how your family would feel about the extra hours you might work or want to check that none of your co-workers would feel hurt or taken advantage of by your decision. The same judgment cannot be made using both the thinking and feeling functions—they are two opposing ways of doing the same thing. A person who has no clear preference for either thinking or feeling will make one judgment one way and another judgment the other way, or will experience conflict while making judgments.

Another function of living is a *perceptive* one. Jung delineated two different patterns in the way we perceive the world around us. A person can use *sensing* function by calling on the five senses to take in information or the *intuitive* function by following hunches, images, or possibilities rather than relying on concrete, observed reality. If you were considering buying an old house, using your sensing function to perceive that house, you would notice the peeling paint, the rotting floor boards, the dampness in the basement, and the leak around the chimney. If I were to look at the same house, using my intuitive function, I might see only how the house would look once the roof was replaced, the walls taken out to make larger rooms, and the yard landscaped. You might not see the potential of the house, and I might not ever notice the damp basement. As was the case for the judgmental functions, sensing and intuition are opposing functions—two incompatible ways of seeing the same thing. A person cannot use both functions simultaneously. When people do not have a clear preference for either sensing or intuition, they may alternate between the two and possibly experience frustration at the varying perceptions.

Type Profiles

Jung ([1921] 1971) combines the two attitudes and the four functions to define eight psychological types: extraverted thinking, feeling, sensing, and intuition; and introverted thinking, feeling, sensing, and intuition. The attitudes and the functions work together. For example, extraverted thinking involves making logical rational judgments about things in the external world, whereas introverted thinking is an inner reflective process. Although Jung cautions us that these are not rigid or exclusive categories, some followers of Jung's theory have objectively compartmentalized the psychological types (for example, see Myers, 1985).

Most people have a *dominant function* or a preferred way of being. If my dominant function is introverted thinking, this means that, given a choice, I will engage in an inner process of thought and reflection. If your dominant function is extraverted sensing, this means that you would prefer to experience real events in the world—do things and see things. This does not mean that either of us is unable or unwilling to use other functions, but rather that this is our favored style or process.

Similarly, most people have an *auxiliary function*. Since we all make judgments and perceive things, the auxiliary function is complementary to the dominant function. If the first preference is judgmental, either through thinking or feeling, then the second preference is perceptive, either through sensing or intuition. For a person whose dominant function is judgmental, the perceptive function provides the information, visions, or images which are to be judged. The judging is the preferred activity. For a person whose dominant function is perceptive, the information or images are first taken in, and judgment follows. The perception is the preferred activity.

These various combinations of preferences can be represented in a profile, thereby maintaining the individuality of the person (Cranton and Knoop, 1995). Figure 3.1 illustrates a profile of psychological type for Sharon. Sharon's dominant function is extraverted intuition, meaning that she prefers to work with visions and possibilities in the external world rather than details acquired through her senses. Her auxiliary function is extraverted thinking, indicating that she will use logic and reason to make judgments about the things she perceives. Sharon is less likely to use her feeling function, to make judgments based on values, but she can do so in some contexts or on certain occasions. She will find it difficult to use her sensing function as it is overshadowed by her preference for intuition. On the inside, however, when Sharon is alone and introspective, she may personalize information gathered through her senses, using introverted sensing—on the introverted side, this preferences is nearly as strong as intuition. Sharon would feel bothered by this process, however, as it is in direct conflict with her strongest preference. Jung calls this the *inferior* function and describes it as mostly unconscious. When we do something that feels completely wrong or foreign to our nature, this may mean that we are using our inferior function.

The use of a profile to represent psychological type preferences allows us considerable flexibility in understanding ourselves or others. While learning and teaching styles inventories are useful and increase awareness of individual differences, the labels often do not quite fit. It seems unlikely that there are just four kinds of learners in the world (for example, see Kolb, 1984). As I discuss in the latter two sections of this chapter, psychological type preferences can be used to understand teaching and learning preferences.

Figure 3.1: Type Profile for Sharon

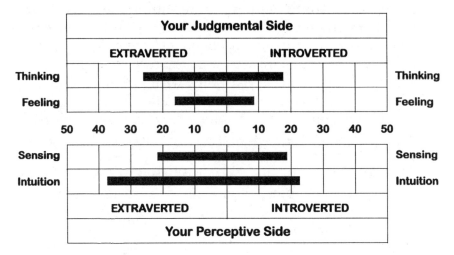

Differentiation

As mentioned above in the description of the psychological type functions, not everyone clearly prefers thinking or feeling, or sensing or intuition. It is tempting to see
this kind of person as well-rounded, but Jung ([1921]
1971) argues that a person must first differentiate the
various components of the psyche and then consciously
develop the functions. He calls this process *individuation*:
"the process by which individual beings are formed and
differentiated; in particular it is the development of the
psychological *individual* as being distinct from the general, collective psychology" (p. 448). The individual way is
never, by definition, a norm. In other words, we become
aware of ourselves, and in doing so, separate our way of
being from that of others. Given that state of self-awareness, we can then deliberately develop various facets of
our personality, albeit with difficulty.

A person who has clear preferences has a differentiated
psyche. A person who does not is still undifferentiated.
This concept applies primarily to the opposing functions:
thinking versus feeling and sensing versus intuition.

Sometimes, when the dominant and auxiliary functions are equally strong, they may also compete with each other. The attitudes, introversion and extraversion, can be similar in strength.

Lack of differentiation appears to the observer as inconsistency or unpredictability. For example, we may not know if the person will make a decision based on reason or values (undifferentiation between thinking and feeling), or if he or she will pay attention to concrete details or the larger picture (undifferentiation between sensing and intuition). This can be disconcerting since we generally prefer knowing what to expect from others. Individuals who have undifferentiated profiles may experience conflict, uncertainty, or discomfort when using those functions for which they have no clear preference. This can lead to feelings of stress, lack of self-confidence, or the avoidance of situations in which the functions would be used. For example, the person who avoids judgments by asking others to make decisions could be undifferentiated between the thinking and feeling functions.

Using psychological type theory as a framework, I review how our individual differences are displayed in the way we teach. In part, this discussion is based on data collected in a research project in which we surveyed about 500 educators on various facets of their preferences (Cranton and Knoop, 1994).

Teaching Style Preferences

During the exchanges we have with learners, our teaching style reveals our beliefs, values, and knowledge about teaching. This style may be conscious, deliberately developed on the basis of experience, or largely unconscious and unarticulated. The literature provides many different ways of distinguishing teaching styles. Heimlich and Norland (1994) review some of the earlier attempts to classify teaching styles: for example, proactive versus reactive; drillmaster, content-centered, instructor-centered, intellect-centered, and person-centered; the behavior-control model, the discovery-learning model, and the rational model. Heimlich and Norland present the Van Tilburg/Heimlich Teaching Beliefs Scale, which categorizes educators as facilitators, enablers, experts, or providers. They also include as a resource the Norland/Heimlich Teaching Values Scale which indicates whether you focus on content, environment, teacher, group, or student.

Elsewhere I describe 12 possible roles that educators may adopt, depending on their teaching style preferences (Cranton, 1992). These roles range from instructor-centered (expert, planner) to facilitator, co-learner, and reformer roles. In another attempt to classify approaches to teaching, I describe subject-oriented (expert), consumer-oriented (facilitator), and reformist (provocateur) styles (Cranton, 1994). In fact, in the adult education literature and in many guides for new faculty (e.g., see Renner, 1983), most discussions of teaching style are based on a continuum that moves from instructor-centered at one pole to learner-centered at the other. Here, although I generally accept this perspective, I also recognize that our teaching techniques may vary, encompassing different styles from the continuum, depending on the context within which we happen to be working. For example, I am more instructor- and subject-oriented when I teach a course in statistics than I am with a group in an adult education program. I also, as we all do, change styles in response to particular groups of learners. Nevertheless, I do not use styles that are discrepant with my nature—if we try to proceed completely in ways that are at odds with our inherent preferences, we appear inauthentic or even foolish.

Thinking Function and Teaching Style

When an educator prefers to use the thinking function, the teaching is likely to be well organized and carefully planned. Judgments are based on logic. Therefore, for example, the course outline and class agendas may be ordered according to the relationships among the concepts in the subject matter rather than student interests or what is valued by the group. Use of the thinking function may lead to a teaching style which is directive, instructor-centered, or subject-oriented, because the teacher likes to have things designed systematically and does this easily. Most of the literature on effective teaching includes organization as a key component of quality (for example, see Abrami and d'Apolonia, 1990).

However, people using the thinking function also like to operate according to well-thought-out principles and procedures. Therefore, given a good reason to be less directive or more learner-centered, this educator may work as hard to implement those principles as she would to prepare a logically structured teaching sequence. Effective implementation of a pedagogical principle can be added to productive transmission of content as a teaching goal.

When thinking is more introverted than extraverted, the educator who prefers this function may be more reflective, introspective, and critical of his own teaching methods. The emphasis on structure, organization, control, and direction is as much a part of the natural teaching style as it is for the more extraverted person, but it is inner-directed and therefore less explicit and not so visible to the learner.

Feeling Function and Teaching Style

When an educator makes judgments based on values, or likes and dislikes, a different teaching style may emerge. Jung ([1921] 1971, p. 354) describes the feeling as "always in harmony with objective values." Instructors who use the feeling function are interested in establishing good rapport with learners and a collaborative learning atmosphere, and display a strong interest in learners as people. The actual content of the course or class can be secondary to encouraging the process of people learning and working together. Group work, discussion, and co-operative projects may characterize the teaching style that is derived from use of the feeling function. This style is widely advocated in the adult education literature, especially by those theorists who are described as humanists (Knowles, 1980). Achieving rapport and facilitating discussion are also commonly listed as attributes of effective instruction in higher education (Centra, 1993).

Use of the feeling function in teaching does not preclude having sound organization of content or other commonly accepted qualities of good teaching. The educator who is interested in making all learners comfortable and happy strives to build in those features which she knows will be helpful to individuals in the group.

When the feeling function is more introverted than extraverted, the value-based judgments are more inner-directed and therefore personalized. The open caring expressed by the extraverted function may be less explicit and more restrained. However, when the educator with this preference works closely with individuals or small groups of learners, the same warm humanistic atmosphere will prevail as for his more extraverted colleague, whose style may seem inappropriate, intense, or overblown to the introverted observer.

Sensing Function and Teaching Style

An educator who uses a perceptive function will gather information or insights and delay judgment. The sensing function focuses on concrete reality, observed experience—using the senses. The teaching style that emerges from this preference is one which encourages experiential learning, learning by doing. Working in real-life situations, laboratories, shops, or otherwise in the field would be approved of by a person who favors the sensing function. Practical skills rather than abstract theories and down-to-earth experiences rather than vague visions are likely to be the goals of teaching and learning. The educational literature from Dewey (1938) onward advocates experiential learning. Three phases in Kolb's (1984) learning cycle are directly related to the importance of concrete experience. Mezirow (1991) bases his theory of transformative learning on the process of making meaning out of experience.

Although the sensing function is perceptive rather than judgmental, an educator who has this as a dominant preference also has an auxiliary judgmental function. It is through this mechanism that he or she organizes content or selects activities to meet the expressed preferences of the learners.

When the sensing function is more introverted than extraverted, experiences and information may be subjectified or personalized. Personal meaning is attached to observations and events. This preference may mean that teaching large classes is uncomfortable or difficult, but in smaller learning groups, the educator displays an unusually sensitive manner. When combined with a preference for the feeling function, an exceptionally caring and responsive teaching style can result.

Intuitive Function and Teaching Style

A preference for the intuitive functions leads to an interest in improving things, bringing about change, and working toward visions of the future. This educator is

innovative, creative, and enthusiastic about new challenges. The favored teaching style can be one of reformer
or provocateur. An educator with this preference possibly
supports learner empowerment, autonomy, and self-directed learning, all of which can be a part of the visionary
role that intuition tends toward. In the adult education
literature, many of the currently promoted approaches to
teaching, such as transformative learning, fall easily into
the domain of the intuitive function. In the work on
effective teaching in higher education, characteristics
such as enthusiasm for the subject and ability to challenge learners are viewed as part of good practice.

When the intuitive preference is complemented by
thinking, the educator uses that function to organize
course material, making judgments about what is appropriate based on logic. When it is accompanied by a secondary preference for feeling, the personal values and
interests of the learners guide the progression of the
teaching process. Both combinations yield different but
equally valued teaching styles.

If the intuitive function is more introverted than extraverted, the images and visions tend to come from
within. The educator follows hunches, knows instinc-
tively when the teaching and learning process is working,
and relates to students in unexpected and inspirational
ways. The use of such intuition leads to an almost inexplicable sixth sense in teaching. The teaching methods
used may be varied, but whether lecture or group work is
chosen, students will have a sense that the educator is in
tune with what is happening.

Authenticity

There is no one best teaching style or most effective way
to work with learners. Each of the styles described here
is valid and valuable; each is advocated in the literature

in some way. Each person can find an appropriate teaching style derived from his or her natural preferences, values, and past experiences. There is little point in a reserved and sensitive educator trying to be a dynamic lecturer in large classes. There is equally little point in someone with an enthusiastic and boisterous personality attempting to repress those characteristics in order to have a quiet classroom. This is not to say that we should not develop our teaching style by expanding and adding to our repertoire, but we should do so only in a way that is congruent with who we are as people. In Chapter Four, I discuss the development of a philosophy of practice, a process of making explicit our style and our reasons for using that style.

Learning Style Preferences

Originally, educational researchers tried to find the best teaching methods that would be effective for all students. Then we realized that people learn in various ways and therefore respond differently to each teaching strategy. Some learning style models center on which of the senses learners prefer to use, and others on the favored learning conditions (Dunn and Dunn, 1977). In the 1970s, considerable energy was devoted to understanding cognitive style—the ways that individuals process and remember information. For example, some people were found to pay more attention to details and others to a whole figure or scene; some people were seen to respond quickly and impulsively to a problem while others pondered the alternatives (see Cranton, 1989, for a fuller explanation of these learner characteristics).

Today, Kolb's (1984) approach to learning style remains the most commonly used model although serious criticisms have arisen (Jarvis, 1987). Kolb defines two continua along which people vary: from learning through concrete experience to learning through reflective obser-

vation; and from learning through abstract conceptualization to learning from active experimentation. These
continua also form phases in a learning cycle. In other
words, as people learn, they go through all phases—experiencing something, reflecting on it, constructing a theory
to explain it, and testing the theory. Along the way, depending on what they are learning or doing, people develop preferences for one part of the cycle or another. This
becomes their learning style.

Brookfield (1990) argues that a number of other characteristics, including personality, are more important in
determining who is going to learn in what way. I propose
that psychological type theory can provide a framework
that incorporates learning style, among other variables,
to allow us to understand how we learn. Based partly on
theory and partly on data collected from nearly 1,000
individuals as one part of a larger research project (Cranton and Knoop, 1994), I relate learning preferences to
psychological type preferences.

Thinking Function and Learning Style

Learners who prefer the thinking function enjoy working with logical and analytical materials. Kolb's learning
phase of abstract conceptualization seems closest to the
operation of the thinking function. That is, learning occurs by generating analytical and conceptual hypotheses
in order to explain information drawn from an experience.
When the course content is not suited to their kind of
judgmental processes, learners with this tendency may
either feel frustrated and out of their depth, or they may
impose their own structure on the material in order to
work with it. Students who are using their thinking
function are well accommodated by the traditional higher
education classroom where the emphasis is on the acquisition of instrumental knowledge through analysis and
logical problem solving.

When the thinking function is more introverted than extraverted, the learning is a subjective process guided by personal thoughts and concepts. It remains logical and analytical, but is inner-oriented rather than focused on external facts and information derived from experiences. Contemplation, reflection, reading, and independent study may be chosen learning activities.

Feeling Function and Learning Style

The feeling function leads people to want to be in agreement with others and their values. Kolb has no comparable process in his learning cycle, but according to Dunn and Dunn's (1977) model of learning conditions, this would result in a strong social need—a preference for working with others. Learning may be most likely to occur through group work, collaboration, networks, discussion circles, or any process in which value-based judgments have a place. Situations in which people are not important might be somewhat distressing; however action might be taken to relieve discomfort, such as setting up informal groups or learning partners. Most of the strategies advocated in the adult education literature fit well with the feeling function.

With a tendency to introversion, learners are less likely to enjoy working with groups, but would rather work alone or with one trusted colleague or partner. The process is still values-based, but is derived from within rather than from people and events in the outside world. To an observer, such a learner may appear to be withdrawn or unpredictable.

Sensing Function and Learning Style

Learning by doing could be the hallmark of this particular style, which demonstrates a preference for learning through practice, in hands-on situations, and by actual experiences. This is congruent with a great deal of the literature on learning; three phases of Kolb's learning cycle, learning from concrete experience, reflective observation (gathering data generated by an experience), and active experimentation all describe the sensing function well. In general, experiential learning is widely recommended. Working with abstract theories or subjective ideas might be difficult for learners with such a preference—concrete examples and illustrations are needed to link concepts to reality. Practical applications take precedence over theory.

A tendency toward introversion brings a personal perspective to the learning process. Experiences assimilated through sense perceptions are subjectified and special meaning is added. The introverted sensing function is less part of the real world, but is still stimulated by it. It is easy for teachers to misinterpret this process, seeing it as a distortion or confusion of facts rather than an internalization of the information.

Intuitive Function and Learning Style

When asked how they prefer to learn, people with extraverted intuition as a dominant function tend to mention independence, autonomy, exploring on their own, and unstructured learning experiences. Through use of their intuitive function, individuals search for fresh outlets and new possibilities in the world. The actual methods used in the learning experience may matter little, as long as intuition is enthusiastically engaged with the content. A negative feature is that this kind of learner may become bored or drop the pursuit if the material appears to offer no more possibilities. Although it may appear chaotic or disorganized to an observer, intuition sparks a creative and active learning style. Research on self-directed learning consistently indicates that self-directed learning readiness is correlated with scores on intuitive scales (Herbeson, 1992). In fact, a perusal of items on instruments designed to measure self-directed learning (for example, Guglielmino, 1977) reveals that many of the items reflect intuition.

When intuition is more introverted than extraverted, the images and visions come from the inner psyche rather than from the real world. Learners with introverted intuition as a dominant function also prefer to learn independently, and otherwise care little about what method is used; however, they do not overtly express the same enthusiasm that the more extraverted person does. Teachers often suspect that learning is not taking place, but the person may be fully engaged in his own mind.

Learner Profiles

In order to differentiate clearly among learning preferences, it was necessary to describe each one separately. However, keep in mind that such distinctions are artificial and no one falls neatly into these categories. Each person learns in a variety of ways. One student may prefer organization and structure, but also may benefit from group work or collaborative projects. Another may enjoy learning by doing, but be equally comfortable reading a book or listening to a lecture. It is a mistake to classify individuals according to one learning style and then try to teach in ways that are in accord with that style. Even if it were possible to do this—and it is not when one works with groups of individuals, all of whom have different preferences—we would be depriving learners of experiencing or developing new strategies. I propose that people have learning profiles, much as they have psychological type profiles. This means that we probably prefer one or more ways of learning, and some processes make us decidedly uncomfortable, but overall, we usually learn in several ways, with slightly varying degrees of success. Figure 3.2 is an example of what such a profile might look

Figure 3.2: Learner Profile for Brett

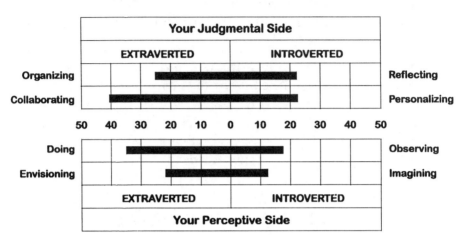

like. The framework is derived from psychological type, and the emphasis is on learning preferences.

Brett's strongest preference is for collaborative learning. Given a choice, he likes to learn in this way, but his choice may also depend on the context or the content of the learning. Brett's second strongest preference is for learning by doing—through practical experiences in the real world. The ideal learning situation for Brett would be a practical, collaborative project. To some extent, he reflects on and personalizes his learning experiences, but imagination is not his strong suit. He probably would not excel at understanding and using metaphors or creating collages.

If we remember that our learners have a profile rather than a style, we can envision how a group may respond to the teaching styles we use. Some individuals may have strong preferences and be uncomfortable in one or more learning modes, as Brett would be in the imaginative style. It is relatively easy to spot such discomfort or difficulty if the class is not too large. Other individuals may be able to work well in most styles, even though they may favor one or two. This gives us a freedom in our selection of teaching approaches that we do not have if we follow a traditional learning style model where it is suggested that educators deliberately address each style.

Summary

Just as human beings differ from one another in their values, beliefs, and past experiences, so too do they differ in the way they teach and learn. No one way is superior to another, even though a particular group or community may value one over the other. Jung's ([1921] 1971) theory of psychological type provides a framework for understanding and appreciating individual differences. Jung describes two attitudes toward the world—extraversion, which is oriented toward things external to the person, and introversion, which is oriented toward the self. These attitudes are focused on four basic functions of living. We use either thinking (logic) or feeling (values) to make judgments, and we perceive the world either by sensing (concrete reality) or intuition (future possibilities). We can create profiles of individuals which reflect their preferences for each of the combinations of attitudes and functions. The use of profiles maintains the uniqueness and complexity of individuals while also revealing patterns and similarities among people.

Using psychological type theory to delineate teaching styles gives us a fresh perspective on the jumble of styles presented in the literature. Use of the thinking function in teaching leads to the creation of a carefully organized, planned, and structured environment with choice of methods and strategies based on logical judgment. The educator's feeling function emphasizes rapport, harmony, and collaboration among people in the learning group. The sensing function focuses on concrete reality and practical experiences in the teaching and learning process. Alternatively, intuition leads to interest in the future, alternative possibilities, change, and reform. Each of these functions may be more or less extraverted or introverted, changing the orientation from outer- to inner-directed. All educators have all functions, but usually prefer to use one or two over the others.

Psychological type theory is equally effective in describing learning preferences. Students who prefer the thinking function look for or create structure and organization in their own learning experiences. The feeling function leads learners to an interest in working in groups or with a partner, and to a desire for a conflict-free learning atmosphere. Students who are using their sensing function appreciate practical and experiential learning and may eschew abstract future-oriented material. Those with the intuitive function search for new possibilities in the learning, usually independently of others. Each of these learning styles can occur anywhere along the continuum of introversion to extraversion.

We can think of students in terms of their learning profile, rather than individuals who learn in only one of a variety of ways. That is, all people learn in different ways, but they may prefer one or two ways over others, and these preferences may vary with the subject matter and the context of the learning. Recognizing this complexity in learning style gives us considerably more freedom in planning for teaching and learning.

Chapter Four

Planning for Teaching and Learning

How do we plan for teaching? First of all, planning a new course may entail research and reading in the subject, and consulting with colleagues who have taught the course. Preparing for a course we have taught many times may involve reviewing the textbook, looking over old notes, and thinking about changes or improvements. Getting ready for tomorrow's class often involves developing handouts or overhead transparencies and going over notes or readings. Sometimes, when time runs short, we grab the course file on the way to class and ad lib our way through a discussion with students, planning and adjusting in action!

Usually planning for teaching and learning is careful and systematic, focusing more on the subject material than the teaching process. However, as workloads increase, preparing for teaching may take a back seat to other demands, especially when research productivity is rewarded over teaching excellence (Smythe, 1995). We count contact hours with students—the amount of time spent in the classroom. We count the number of students in classes, and we count the number of articles published or the number of committees served on. But planning for teaching is something many of us do on the weekend or in the evening. Rarely do we include planning when we describe our work.

In our rush to get things done and to cope with the pressures of academic life, it is not often that we have the opportunity to think about what teaching means to us.

How do we view our practice? What is it about teaching that is important to us? What is a good class? Yet, it is from this kind of thinking about teaching that the planning process flows. As mentioned in Chapter One, people have recently begun to write about *the scholarship of teaching* (Boyer, 1990; Paulsen and Feldman, 1995). Although the definition is a matter of debate in the literature, Rice (1991), for example, describes scholarship as having four dimensions—the advancement, application, representation, and integration of knowledge. This implies that teaching is neither a mechanical process nor routine in nature—thinking about what teaching means to us is an integral part of planning.

There are several levels and types of planning for teaching. Getting ready for tomorrow's class is critical. Preparing a course outline or working on a larger scale to develop a program is equally important. Developing a personal philosophy of practice provides the grounding for all other planning, but it may be the component to which we dedicate the least time. Being informed and up to date in our discipline runs parallel to preparation for teaching. Recently, it has been argued that we need to take a more holistic approach to academic work, integrating teaching preparation with research and expertise in the discipline, rather than viewing them as competitors for our precious time (for example, see Gaff, 1994 and Johnston, 1996). In this chapter I describe three levels of planning for teaching and learning. At the broadest level, articulating a philosophy of practice, I suggest the kinds of activities faculty can engage in to increase their awareness of what it is they value in teaching. I also discuss the process of critically examining a philosophy of practice. At the next level, I review the procedures for curriculum development—course or program planning. Finally, I consider the creation of learning experiences for classes—how to get ready for tomorrow's session.

Articulating a Philosophy of Practice

The phrase sounds intimidating—"a philosophy of practice." Recently, an educator who was enroled in one of my graduate courses spent several frustrating weeks trying to express her philosophy of practice. I suggested to her, "Forget about education for a while, tell me about your philosophy of parenting. What does it mean to you to be a good parent?" She did this easily and then was able to arrive at and articulate her view of herself as a teacher. As educators, we need to be aware of what being an educator means to us. We need to be able to express this to ourselves, to our students, and to our colleagues. Our personal philosophy of practice provides the foundation for all of the decisions we make about teaching. Educational practice without a rationale or a mission makes us technicians rather than professionals.

Brookfield (1986) suggests that a philosophy of practice should include at least three elements: a clear definition of the activity, a number of general purposes derived from the definition, and a set of criteria by which the success of the practice can be judged. In other words, what exactly is a teacher in a higher educational setting? What are the purposes or goals of such work? How do we know when we have succeeded? This is still a general description. It is difficult, and perhaps not all that useful except to theorists, to define teaching or list the goals of teaching in general when our work varies so much across disciplines and contexts, and among people of different personalities and backgrounds. The process needs to be personal, but still retain the essential elements.

We should be able to respond to the following kinds of questions about our own teaching in our own context:

- How would I describe my teaching?
- What are my overall goals in teaching?

- What are my roles in the classroom, the community, and society?
- How would I describe the learners I work with?
- What methods do I usually use and why do I use them?
- What makes a good course for me? A bad course?
- What makes a good class? A bad class?

These questions may be difficult to answer on a first pass. Articulating a philosophy of practice requires increased self-awareness, dialogue with others, and critical questioning of our beliefs and values.

Increasing Self-Awareness as an Educator

Describing a philosophy of practice means that we first need to be aware of ourselves as educators, that is, what it is that we do and why it is that we do it. As we carry out the daily tasks of teaching and academic life, we usually do not think about our goals and our rationale for one method over another. However, the process of increasing self-awareness must be on-going. Each individual may follow a different path during this process: some people like to keep journals, others talk to their colleagues about their work, and still others quietly review their class on the drive home from work. To aid in the search for self-knowledge, I suggest examining three areas: one's personal values, one's social attitudes, and one's knowledge about teaching. These areas are derived directly from Mezirow's (1991) three kinds of meaning perspectives (ways of understanding the world).

At a personal level, we should think about the following questions:

- When and why did I decide to be a teacher?
- What personal needs does my teaching fulfill?
- What aspects of my personality suit the teaching role?
- What do I like and dislike about teaching?

- What anxieties or fears do I have about teaching?
- Am I a good teacher?

At a social level, it is important to consider our reactions to these kinds of questions:

- Was my decision to go into higher education influenced by my social or cultural background?
- How are college and university teachers viewed in my family? Among my friends? In my community?
- How do my students view and value teachers?
- How does my institution view and value teachers?
- Do people treat me differently when they know what I do?
- How do the media portray faculty?

What we know about teaching, either through experience, reading, professional development activities, or formal courses, forms an important component of our self-awareness as educators. Some questions to consider are:

- How have I gained my knowledge of teaching?
- How often do I think about teaching?
- What is my teaching style and how has it developed?
- What are the most important things I know about teaching?
- How do I prefer to learn?
- What workshop or seminar on teaching would I like to take?

Talking about teaching with colleagues, students, family, and friends is another way to help to clarify one's perspective.

Dialogue with Others

Teaching tends to be a private activity. We rarely invite colleagues or others into our classrooms or discuss with our peers questions such as those listed above. At best, we may comment to a colleague that we had a good class or discuss the characteristics of specific students we share. This reluctance is especially ironic given that we advocate discussion as a means to further our students' learning. So, how do we develop an understanding of our practice without talking about it?

A good number of the professional development offerings at colleges and universities include activities based on dialogue among peers. For example, Amundsen, Gryspeerdt, and Moxness (1993) describe discussion groups which were used effectively in McGill University's Centre for Teaching and Learning program. Faculty can engage in more dialogue about teaching in several ways. For example, they can:

- participate in professional development workshops;
- initiate discussion groups;
- join discussion groups on the Internet (e.g., with the Society for Teaching and Learning in Higher Education);
- talk openly and informally about teaching in the work room or the faculty club;
- bring up items related to teaching goals at department meetings;
- invite colleagues into their classrooms.

Critical Questioning

In order for reflection and discussion to lead to growth and development, critical questioning of our philosophies of practice is necessary. Elsewhere, I present a model of professional development that is founded on critical self-reflection (Cranton, 1996a). We can increase our self-awareness of our values and beliefs about teaching. We can engage in discussion with others about teaching. But if we want our philosophy of practice to be a fluid and

Table 4.1: Critical Questions about Teaching

Content Reflection	What did I do in class?
	What did I do to foster learning?
	What are the goals and rationale for this curriculum?
Process Reflection	How did I come to choose to do that in class?
	How did I come to foster learning in this way?
	How did I/we come to have these goals and rationale?
Premise Reflection	Why is what I do in class important?
	Why is it important that I foster learning?
	Why is it important that we have goals and rationale?

evolving perspective, we must also continually question ourselves.

In Chapter One, I describe three kinds of reflection—content (what happened?), process (how did it come to be this way?), and premise (why is this important?)—that can be used to understand teaching. This categorization is a part of Mezirow's (1991) theory of transformative learning. Critical questioning, especially of the premises of our beliefs, can transform our perspectives on teaching practice. In Table 4.1, I list some critical questions about teaching. These questions can be reflected on in private, talked about informally with others, and used as a focus in discussion groups. The questioning of premises is especially important in developing a philosophy of practice.

Curriculum Development

Curriculum development, or program and course planning, is what most faculty think of when they consider planning for teaching and learning. The task can vary in complexity, from simply putting together a course outline based on previous years' experiences to developing a new program altogether. Regardless of whether it is a course or a program, new or taught many times, curriculum development is likely to include at least five basic components:

- clarifying the rationale;
- setting goals;
- ordering learning experiences;
- choosing methods; and
- designing evaluations of the teaching and learning process (Cranton, 1989).

These components may not be considered in such an orderly fashion, and students may or may not participate in any or all of them, but they are nearly always discernible in any curriculum development process. We may not always be conscious of going through this process, especially as we gain more experience as teachers. More importantly, we may not always consider why we make the choices we do. At this point, a considered, articulated philosophy of practice can act as a guideline. When we ask, "Why am I including this topic?" or "Why am I choosing that method?" a clear philosophy of practice provides the rationale.

Clarifying the Rationale

All too often, faculty begin to write a course outline or select a textbook before thinking about the reasons for or the values underlying the learning experience. A written rationale forms an important part of curriculum—students, colleagues, administrators, and potential employers are thereby informed as to the nature and basis of the learning experience. The format and content of a curriculum rationale varies, depending on the nature and context of the course. It may include:

- the intent of the course;
- why people would take the course;
- how the course fits into the broader program;
- the general approach that will be used;
- a description of the instructor's style or philosophy; and
- special circumstances or constraints.

The rationale need not be lengthy—it should familiarize the student with what will happen in the course and explain why the course is constructed as it is. In some settings, learners may participate in formulating the rationale for their course. Figure 4.1 gives two excerpts from curriculum rationales.

Setting Goals

The traditional approach to curriculum development calls for the selection and statement of observable or measurable objectives. However, as I discuss in Chapter One, of the different kinds of learning only one can be readily expressed in terms of measurable objectives. The faculty member who works with instrumental knowledge can state such curriculum goals as:

> Upon completion of this course, the learner will be able to conduct a regression analysis with at least three dependent variables using SPSSPC+.

But when we are facilitating communicative knowledge or fostering emancipatory learning, the use of behavioral objectives is less appropriate. Many educators who support a conventional approach to instructional design reject this argument; indeed, I myself took the traditional stance in the past (Cranton, 1989). But, the recent break in education from the pervasive scientific paradigm has opened up new ways of approaching teaching and learning (for example, see Kincheloe, 1991).

Figure 4.1: Excerpts from Curriculum Rationales

Example 1: Introductory Statistics

We hope that you will develop a conceptual understanding of the statistical analyses commonly used in educational research, including the appropriateness of various analyses for the research question and the type of data. This will help you to be informed readers of the educational literature.

You will acquire the skills needed to analyze data in a variety of ways, using SPSSPC. This will enable you to manage your own thesis or project data or to work with others on research projects that include data analysis.

Approach:

As most of you know, we believe as educators that it is our responsibility to encourage self-directed learning and critical thinking. Since statistics is an area that is new to you, technical in nature, and also anxiety-provoking for some people, we have made the initial decisions regarding the topics, objectives, and agenda for the course. We expect, however, as we proceed and you gain expertise with the content, that some of our initial decisions will be questioned and revised. This is *our* course; we have the flexibility and freedom to make of it what we wish.

All sessions will be participatory—through discussion, group activities, and computer projects. At the same time, we hope to share our expertise in and enthusiasm for statistics with you.

Example 2: Instructional Design

Goal:

The goal of Instruction Design II is to provide you with an opportunity to learn more about teaching. This could include practicing presentation skills, constructing tests, planning your courses for the fall, or any of the man other aspects of the complex process of working with learners.

You are adult learners. Therefore ....

- I want this experience to be relevant to your own work and your setting.
- I expect that you will become interested and actively involved in the learning process.
- I respect your learning needs.
- I expect that you will want responsibility for decision-making about your own learning.

- I appreciate the constraints and responsibilities that you have outside our classroom.

- I assume that you will want to participate in the evaluation of your learning.

- I will provide expertise and resources for your learning.

Procedure:

As in any institutionalized teaching and learning setting, there are several constraints within which we must work. Such constraints should be made clear from the beginning ...

- We need to work together for a certain number of hours, at specified times.

- We are working on the topics that come under the umbrella of the course descriptions.

- We need to submit grades to the university.

These constraints are minimal and give us plenty of freedom to engage in meaningful and exciting learning.

Topics:

This course is intended to provide an opportunity for you to explore the topics related to course planning and implementation that are of interest and useful for you. I recognize the tremendous variety of settings within which you work, and your varied backgrounds. I also recognize that various topics are more or less interesting and useful to different people. I hope to be able to arrange, with you, an agenda that contains your interests and meet your needs. You have been teaching now for a minimum of a year, and certainly have clear ideas about what you want to learn. My job is to provide the resources, expertise, guidance, and feedback that facilitate your learning.

We will hold our first session as a planning session in which you discuss and select topics. Some people may want to pursue individual projects, and present them to or discuss them with peers; others may want to have structured sessions, led by me, on specific topics. All of these possibilities are open to us.

Evaluation:

For the evaluation of your learning, I ask you to let me know what you plan to do, fairly early on in the summer. I will meet with you individually to discuss your plans. I will give you as much feedback as you like while you work on your projects. I expect you to set your own criteria for your learning, and to participate in the evaluation process.

In the communicative or emancipatory domains, course goals may read like this:

- Learners will increase their professional self-awareness through discussion with others.
- Learners will develop an appreciation for the values held by individuals from a different culture.
- Learners will critically question the assumptions they hold about gender differences.
- Learners will understand how to use a visual art form to express themselves.

To varying degrees, students can be involved in setting curriculum goals. If they are newcomers to the subject, they will obviously be unable to set goals alone, but may still be involved in some of the decision making. When students have acquired background and experience in the discipline, they may become deeply immersed in this aspect of the planning. Large class sizes make student participation in planning difficult, but not impossible, unless the class has over 100 students. Requirements to submit course outlines before the first class can also prevent student participation in planning.

Ordering Learning Experiences

The way in which course topics or learning experiences are sequenced varies with the type of knowledge involved. The structure of knowledge in some subjects is inherently logical, either hierarchical or linear. In other subjects, the structure is web-like, with concepts related to each other in a variety of ways. Sometimes, the learning sequence is more like a spiral, as students cycle back to certain concepts while progressing upwards to gain expertise. When learning is emancipatory, the order of the experiences inevitably varies from one individual to another.

Traditional sequencing strategies in the domain of instrumental knowledge and technical skills include task analysis and procedural analysis (Bloom and others, 1956; Gagné, 1977; Krathwohl and others, 1964). In task analysis, learning is sequenced from least to most complex. Care is taken to ensure that students acquire all prerequisite knowledge and skills before moving on to subsequent topics. Therefore, the instructor first must analyze the content of a course to determine which concepts must be learned ahead of others (see Cranton, 1989 for examples). Task analysis is ideal when the structure of knowledge in the discipline is hierarchical, as in mathematics, statistics, and most sciences.

In procedural analysis, learning is sequenced to follow the order required to perform the skill. When the student is learning how to repair a small engine or how to set up an intravenous drip efficiently, the task has a natural order. The teacher reviews the task, breaks it into its components, and sequences the learning experience in the order of the performance itself (see Cranton, 1989 for examples). Procedural analysis is called for when technical and psychomotor skills are being taught.

Unfortunately, task and procedural analysis are still often applied to disciplines in which the structure of the knowledge is neither hierarchical nor based on the performance of manual skills. Instructional design and educational technology—the application of methods of instrumental knowledge to all teaching and learning—has had a profound impact on education. To take but one example, Woiceshyn (1992, p. 86) argues that "knowledge in any field forms a hierarchy with concrete facts as the base" and "interest...cannot be the organizing principle because students may be interested in questions they are not ready to learn. Instead the hierarchical nature of the subject determines the structure of the course." This statement is made in criticism of business policy courses that organize learning around case studies.

When the subject area is neither hierarchical nor linear in structure, the learning experiences may be ordered in a variety of ways. Faculty can consider:

- following an historical sequence;
- progressing from basic to specialized material;
- providing the overall schema first, then tying ideas and concepts into that framework;
- beginning with topics of greatest interest to learners;
- drawing a map of the associations among concepts and clustering concepts according to their similarities; and
- responding to practical considerations such as the schedule of a field site or a cooperating business.

Students and teachers will perceive the structure of knowledge in any field differently from one another—as we move from novice to expert in an area, our notion of how concepts are related to each other changes. Therefore, faculty must also be aware of the learner's perspective when they are planning. Learners can be involved in the ordering of learning experiences. At the most basic level, they can give feedback as to whether or not the sequence of presentation of material seemed appropriate and helped them learn. When students are more familiar with the course content, they can work in teams to plan the sequence of components of the course or even the entire course. Sometimes, individuals or small groups within a class can work with different sequences. When students follow different paths—working on various group projects, for example—they can further stimulate each other's learning by exchanging ideas and insights.

Choosing Methods

The choice of teaching methods is based primarily on the kind of learning we are hoping to encourage. Even though the temptation often is to stay with familiar methods and avoid the risks of trying something new, it is critical that the strategy be in tune with the learning. I remember trying to learn a complex mathematical concept by reading about it rather than working through the proofs and problems. I have seen teachers talking to a group about group dynamics without ever engaging in group work. At the simplest level, students need to do what they are learning.

There are many ways of classifying teaching methods in order to match them to various purposes. Heimlich and Norland (1994), for example, describe presentation, experiential, discovery, game, media, and teacher-absent methods. Each method in this framework is used for a specific purpose. Earlier, I presented a system of instructor-centered, interactive, individualized, and experiential methods (Cranton, 1989) in order to relate methods to Bloom's (1956), Krathwohl's (1964), and Simpson's (1966) learning taxonomies. For our purposes here, if we categorize teaching methods as instructor-centered, facilitative, and reformist, we can then see how these categories relate to the kinds of human interests and knowledge described by Habermas (1971) (see Chapter One). Some specific methods may fall into more than one group, depending on how they are used.

Instructor-centered methods are those in which the communication travels primarily from teacher to student. Lectures and demonstrations are the classic examples. Also included are modularized or distance education techniques when the information is conveyed from the teacher through another medium to the student.

When facilitative methods are used, the direction of communication is at least equally distributed between educator and learners, but often there is more learner than teacher talk. The facilitator coordinates, manages, guides, and helps. Group work, group projects, discussions, role playing, simulations, and games are methods that fall into this category. When distance education

Table 4.2: Matching Methods to Kinds of Knowledge

Kind of Knowledge	Teaching Method	Purpose
Instrumental	Instructor-centered	Transmitting knowledge
Communicative	Facilitative	Enhancing understanding of the self and social norms
Emancipatory	Reformist	Fostering individual empowerment and social change

utilizes group work and discussion, it, too, can be facilitative.

Reformist methods have as their goal individual development and empowerment, and social change. Communication is two-directional, but of a different nature. The teacher challenges, questions, and stimulates critical reflection. Critical incidents, dialogue journals, role playing, group projects, discussion groups, and field or clinical experiences can be reformist methods.

In Table 4.2, I relate teaching methods to the kinds of knowledge we hope students will attain. In Chapter One, I describe these kinds of knowledge in terms of the goals of higher education. Here, we can see how the same framework guides our choice of instructional strategies.

Instructional materials—books, articles, models, overhead transparencies, computer software, and videotapes—can be used in conjunction with any method. A reading may accompany a lecture, precede a discussion group, or provide a provocative resource for critical reflection. Some materials, used alone, allow for little interaction. Watching a videotape, for example, is passive. However, a videotape can act as a stimulus for either communicative or emancipatory learning if used in conjunction with facilitative or reformist methods. In other words, the materials do not determine the kind of learning promoted.

As is the case for each of the components of curriculum planning, learners can be involved in the selection of teaching methods. Often, learners have strong preferences for one or more methods and will gladly provide that information. It is a simple matter to ask a group whether they would prefer to do this or that during the next class, and this gives students a sense of involvement and responsibility for their learning. It is more difficult to give students complete responsibility for methods selection, but this can be done in some circumstances. Generally, the more decision-making power students have, the greater is their commitment to class activities. However, we should also note Brookfield's (1995) caution against never challenging learners to work outside of their preferred style.

Evaluating Learning and Teaching

The selection of the method of evaluating learning is based on the nature of the expected learning. Whatever it is that we and our students anticipate knowing or doing as a result of a learning experience should be what we evaluate. Whether this is the operation of equipment on a forestry site, reading technical reports in a second language, or gaining personal autonomy, the evaluation strategy needs to match the learning process. Answering multiple-choice questions has nothing or little to do with equipment operation. Writing essays is an inefficient way to evaluate the retention of factual material.

Evaluation techniques are commonly classified as objectively or subjectively scored. For our purposes here, I add the category of learner self-evaluation. The process is different enough to be treated separately. I also refer to subjectively *rated* strategies rather than subjectively scored. To rate is to estimate the value or worth of something; to score is to have a specified value in points. When a student's work is subjectively evaluated, we are estimating its value or worth.

Objectively scored evaluations are those in which there is one right answer to each question. In that case, using an answer key, two people arrive at the same score, unless a counting error occurs. Multiple-choice tests are the most common form of objectively scored evaluations. They efficiently assess students' recognition of facts and definitions, and are especially useful in large classes. Other objectively scored formats include true-false items, matching items, and short answer questions where only one answer is considered correct.

Subjectively rated evaluations are those in which the quality of performance is judged. Criteria exist, but the judgment is nevertheless subjective. Two people interpreting the same performance often do not agree on the quality. Essay tests are the most familiar form of subjectively rated evaluation. They are commonly used to judge complex and qualitative learning. The evaluations of an actual performance—a dance, for example, or the product of a performance, such as creating a weld—are also subjectively rated. Oral tests are less frequently used.

Learner self-evaluations are those in which the student judges and reports on the quality of his or her learning. They are almost always subjectively rated, but the process is markedly different from teacher-directed assessments. The student gains self-evaluation skills, as well as exposure to the content. Increased confidence, critical reflection, self-direction, and personal autonomy are further goals of self-evaluation. Common evaluative formats include journals, log books, essays, life stories, and discussions.

Table 4.3: Matching Evaluation Strategies to Kinds of Learning

Kind of Learning	Evaluation Strategy	Purpose
Instrumental	Objectively-scored	Judging the quantity of knowledge acquired
Communicative	Subjectively-rated	Rating the quality of understanding of the self and social norms
Emancipatory	Learner self-evaluation	Considering the degree of individual empowerment or social change

In Table 4.3, I relate evaluation strategies to the kinds of learning being judged. Teachers working with instrumental knowledge may not use objectively scored evaluations exclusively. For example, laboratory work often has a subjective component, and where critical thinking is being encouraged, subjectively rated formats may be more appropriate. I discuss this dimension of instrumental knowledge in Chapter Five.

I do argue, however, that objectively scored tests are not a valid way to evaluate communicative knowledge, which is interpretive in nature. Neither can they be used for emancipatory knowledge, which is both personal and interpretive. There are no right answers in these domains of learning.

The evaluation of teaching is always subjectively rated as knowledge of teaching is communicative in nature. Student ratings of the quality of instruction are used in colleges and universities across North America, both for formative or improvement purposes and summative or administrative decisions. Although their reliability and validity has been well established during three decades of research, student ratings focus on only one dimension of teaching—learners' perceptions of their teacher's class-room behavior. Examples of other useful strategies include:

- peer review of course materials;
- comments from instructional development consultants;
- collegial observations of teaching;
- comments and letters from alumni;
- reviews from employers of graduates; and,
- documentation of student learning.

Self-evaluation of teaching, like learner self-evaluation, continually takes place as we critically reflect on our practice. This kind of evaluation focuses on our growth and development as educators. Although self-evaluation is usually informal, it can also be formalized for consideration as a legitimate assessment. Centra (1993) recommends that self-reports be used rather than self-ratings, arguing that research shows self-ratings are often inflated and perhaps invalid. Self-reports are open-ended and descriptive, therefore allowing for the inclusion of questions, reflections, and, indeed, bragging about good work!

Recently, there has been a move toward the use of teaching portfolios or dossiers in which these kinds of data are collected over a person's career (Mullins and Cannon, 1991). The dossier includes all evaluative information and documents courses taught and students advised. Ideally, one's philosophy of teaching is also described. The teaching dossier is described in more detail in Chapter Eight.

Preparing Learning Experiences

In Chapters Five, Six, and Seven, I provide detailed descriptions of techniques and strategies for each of instrumental, communicative, and emancipatory learning.

In the first part of this chapter, I encourage faculty to articulate their philosophy of teaching. The planning of the curriculum for a course or program is then derived from one's philosophy. Included in that planning process is the selection of teaching methods. Now I turn to some points to consider in the planning and preparation of learning experiences for individual classes. What shall we do tomorrow?

Regardless of which method—for example, discussion, lecture, field experience, or group projects—has been selected, the following planning guidelines can be helpful in the preparation of each session.

Purpose

The purpose of each session should be clear in the minds of both the teacher and the learners. Ideally, everyone involved, learners and teacher, agree on the purpose. Little is accomplished if the educator's plan is to encourage critical thinking while the students' goal is to copy down facts for an examination. What topics will be discussed, what the learning goals are, and what process will be followed to reach those goals need to be clearly stated for each class and for each activity in longer classes.

There are several ways of clarifying the purpose of learning experiences. Specific goals or objectives can be presented both verbally and in writing at the beginning of a session. An agenda can be distributed. A content-based outline can accompany a lecture. The goals, agenda, or outline can be displayed on an overhead projector, handed out on paper, posted on flip chart paper, and discussed with the class. Even in a 50-minute session, five minutes devoted to the purpose of the session will ensure that the remaining 45 minutes are more organized and productive.

I have already noted (in Chapter Three) that educators and learners with different psychological type preferences have varying likes and dislikes in structure and organization. So, for more intuitive teachers, for example, an agenda or outline may clash with their natural tendency to let things flow as they respond spontaneously to what occurs in each class. While some students are comfortable in this situation, others will be annoyed. A clearly stated purpose will help those learners who find it useful and can remain in the background for the others. This way, the choice is theirs.

Flexibility

Despite the importance of pre-planning of goals, agendas, or outlines, it is equally important to allow oneself to abandon the plan when the situation demands it. For the teacher who is most comfortable with structure, flexibility can be built into the plan itself by leaving extra time open or preparing several optional plans to be followed, depending on how the class transpires. For the teacher who relies less on organized teaching, flexibility is natural and need not be planned for.

Changes in direction, focus, or plan within an individual session may take place in response to a student reaction, a new insight on the part of the teacher, or an unusual event that occurs in a project, demonstration, or field experience. For students who rely on the pre-determined structure of a class agenda or plan, it is important to make such changes explicit, allowing them to reorient themselves to the shift. This can be done simply, by saying, for example, "We were actually on item 4 on the agenda, but our discussion has led us to an interesting point related to tomorrow's topic."

Authenticity

It is tempting to model ourselves on an entertaining, dynamic lecturer or try to adopt the non-judgmental style of an experienced counselor, but all we do is look foolish if we are not ourselves in the classroom. Similarly, we need to encourage learners to be themselves throughout their learning experiences. In planning a class, it is important to consider our own characteristics and preferences, as well as those of our students, and ensure that none of us are forced into uncomfortable or artificial roles.

I once planned a rather lengthy lecture on a topic that was new to the group I was working with as it seemed to be the best way to provide an overview of theoretical information. I was very involved with and interested in the theory, but I did not take into account that I am not comfortable lecturing. After 15 minutes of rather boring and stilted talk, I switched to a more open discussion. Even though the students were not familiar with the theory, the discussion was energetic and the theoretical points were all introduced quite nicely.

On another occasion, I used a debate format that had been successful on previous occasions without considering that many learners in the group were new to higher education, unfamiliar with debating, and lacking in self-confidence when expressing their opinions. When I realized my mistake, I quickly changed the formal debate to a more informal game.

Interaction and Involvement

Everyone who has listened to an hour-long speech will have noticed how attention slips in and out, regardless of the interest in the topic and the quality of the speaker. Learning is not a spectator sport. No matter what method is being used, it is crucial to plan for some form of learner interaction or involvement. In traditional lectures, students maintain their involvement by taking notes, which are used later for review and preparation for examinations. While this works well for some kinds of learning, primarily the acquisition of facts and information, other ways of increasing involvement can easily be incorporated into class planning. Even when groups are large, say, over 100 students, individuals need to be actively and meaningfully involved in the learning experience.

Students can always form pairs or small groups, even in a lecture theater, and discuss an issue, respond to a question, or solve a problem. Such an activity can take five or 45 minutes, depending on the length of the class and the purpose of the interaction. Students may or may not report back to the larger group.

Role plays, debates, simulations, and games can be built into many class plans. Even in a large group, one-half of the class can take one side of an issue, and one-half the other side, and spend a few minutes shouting their arguments from one side of the room to the other. When students become familiar with such activities, great energy and enthusiasm is generated in a short period of time.

Questioning, and especially critical questioning, increases involvement even for those individuals who do not respond aloud to such questions. Questions based on process or premise reflection ("How did things get to be this way?" "Why do we care about this in the first place?") make everyone stop and think for a minute, and thinking is involvement.

Entertainers and public speakers often ask, "Who is here from Arkansas? from Canada?" People raise their hands and look around to see who else shares their background. This is planned involvement. In small groups, it is easy to bring learners' backgrounds, experiences, and opinions into discussions. In large classes, brief surveys can also be conducted using a show of hands, a shouting out of responses, or notations on index cards (collected and referred to in the next class).

Variety

Being flexible and deliberately planning for learner involvement automatically produces variety in the pace and style of the class. Learners with different psychological type preferences and learning styles favor different approaches, so to some extent, we meet more individual needs by varying the nature of class activities. On the other hand, this also means that a good portion of the class is not being considered at any one time.

Perhaps a more reasonable rationale for using a variety of activities and changing the pace of instruction is to maintain everyone's interest, teacher and learners, by engaging in different experiences. A year or two ago, I taught a class of college teachers in an instructors' certification program. Without exception, they expressed a preference for group work, so group work we did. After several classes, they came to tell me, rather sheepishly, that they were tired of group work. We needed to vary the nature of the activities.

When planning a class, we need to think back—how often have I used that approach? Is this the same thing as we did during the last class? It is important always to try something different, for our own sakes as well as for our students, even if it is only a brief break in a routine.

Challenge and Support

I recently heard of a teacher who bragged that her students hated her. "They learn more that way," she argued. One hopes that what she meant is that she challenges her students. Challenge is important, but equally important is a balance between challenge and support. Brookfield (1990, p. 207) argues that "striving to achieve an equilibrium (ever changing though this may be) between these two forces is crucial."

If we only affirm students' perceptions, they may never clear up misapprehensions and question or explore alternatives. However, support and respect for our students is central to our professional practice. To plan ahead for a balance of challenge and support is impossible as we cannot predict just how students will respond and must be free to react to the moment. We can, however, plan a balance between activities that are fun, easy, and rewarding for everyone, and those that are more difficult and challenging. We can deliberately mix praise with critical questioning. We can set up activities in which learners support each other as a group, contrasted with activities that encourage debate and competition. When preparing a class, we need to look at our plan in the light of supporting and challenging learners.

Closure

Equally important to planning the beginning of a class—its purposes and goals—is planning the end, coming to closure. Usually, this takes the form of a short summary and integration of ideas discussed during the class. Relating the topics to the next class or to other parts of the course can form a part of the closure to a session. Asking questions that arise from class can encourage reflection between sessions. Either the teacher may be responsible for closure or this responsibility can rotate among the group. Having students provide the summary and integration or ask the critical question has the added benefit of increasing their involvement.

Closure is also critical following group work, role plays, simulations, or any of the interactive methods. Following group work or small group discussion, it is useful to have groups briefly report on the results of their work so that everyone benefits from their insights and ideas. However, this may not be possible in larger groups. After such activities as role plays and simulations, closure provides an opportunity to relate the activity to the goals of the session. Perhaps even more important, it allows for the expression of the emotions brought to the surface by the activity. Careful debriefing is essential to the use of techniques in which personal feelings are involved.

Summary

Planning for teaching and learning involves many activities, ranging from the immediate, such as preparing a daily agenda for class, to the overarching, such as defining a philosophy of teaching. All levels of planning are equally significant in promoting meaningful teaching and learning experiences. The daily agenda is based on the course curriculum which, in turn, is derived from the underlying philosophy of practice as it applies to the subject.

Developing a philosophy of practice may be the most neglected aspect of planning. Fortunately, it is becoming more common to include such a statement in applications for promotion and to be asked for one when seeking a position. A philosophy of practice is, simply, what it means to us to be a teacher. In order to reflect on this question, we can ask ourselves personal, social, and knowledge-based questions about teaching. We can talk to colleagues and others about our practice. We can be critical of ourselves by questioning what we do, how we came to do things this way, and why it is important in the first place.

Most faculty are more familiar with curriculum development or course planning than they are with describing their philosophy of practice. A curriculum has a rationale, goals or objectives, a certain sequence of events, a planned methodology, and evaluation strategies. Learners can be involved in any or all stages of course planning.

The daily or weekly planning of classes becomes easier when we are clear about our philosophy of practice and have a good curriculum. The details of daily planning are somewhat dependent on the nature of the knowledge one is working with, and therefore on the teaching methods being used. Nevertheless, some guidelines are relevant to most classes. Having a clear purpose and the ability to be flexible helps both those learners who prefer structure and those who like to follow possibilities as they arise. Being true to oneself is as important for the teacher as for the learners. Meaningful learning depends on involvement, which needs to be built into each class plan. Variety increases involvement. How to achieve the critical balance between challenging and supporting students should be considered in every class. Finally, classes and activities within classes should come to closure.

Chapter Five

Transmitting Instrumental Knowledge and Technical Skills

Originating in the twelfth century, universities traditionally have been institutions dedicated to the pursuit of knowledge for its own sake. Students absorbed this knowledge by sitting at the feet of their teachers as they explored the great questions of the world. On the other hand, colleges, a very recent development, were intended primarily to perform a service role—that of educating people to take their places in the workforce. However, the idea of what a university is or should be has changed dramatically in response to changes in society (see Chapter Two), and some of the distinctions between colleges and universities have become blurred. Nevertheless, the historical traditions of the university are still very much alive.

As discussed in Chapter One, in the 18th century, reason and the scientific approach replaced mysticism as the primary mode of viewing the world. With the Age of Enlightenment, reason ruled as it became accepted that the solution of the world's ills would be found through the acquisition and application of instrumental knowledge. World peace, eradication of crime, and full understanding of the human psyche were to be made possible by the application of rational thought. Universities, as purveyors of society's knowledge, were held to be responsible for encouraging and developing rational thought among an elite. Although we no longer believe that the solutions to all social, political, economic, and environmental problems can be found in instrumental knowledge, it will always remain a critical and essential component of our world. Human organ transplantation, worldwide flight, and instant global communication are all products of instrumental knowledge and technical skills.

Despite new demands to be responsive to business and industry, and accountable to the public, universities and colleges will always have a major role to play in the pursuit of pure knowledge. The delivery of that knowledge to others is one vital way in which higher education serves society. Thus, one goal of higher education is the transmission of instrumental knowledge and technical skills.

How is this goal met? Today as we walk through a college or university building, we are likely to see professors talking to large groups of students. The lecture, and in the sciences, the lecture accompanied by laboratory experience, is the most commonly employed strategy for transmitting knowledge. This is the method with which we are most familiar and comfortable, and it is often the best teaching strategy for delivering knowledge. However, it certainly need not be the only method.

In this chapter, I explore three ways of transmitting instrumental knowledge and technical skills—lectures and demonstrations, problem-based learning, and experiential learning. For each, I provide guidelines for when to use the strategy and how to use it effectively. I then discuss the importance of critical thinking in the instrumental domain and propose that critical thinking can and should be encouraged, regardless of the teaching strategies being used.

Lectures and Demonstrations

Why a lecture? Why a demonstration? Aren't students capable of reading the same information in a textbook?

Can't they learn by discovery and experimentation? Our rationale for choosing a teaching method must be clear and justifiable. We need to be especially aware of the reasons for using an instructor-centered lecture or demonstration as these methods are often selected simply because they are the most familiar.

Brookfield (1990) lists five common and worthy reasons for choosing to lecture. These include the need to:

- establish the broad outlines of a body of material, including contrasting schools of thought;
- set guidelines for independent study outside of the classroom;
- model intellectual attitudes, such as critical thinking;
- stimulate interest through animation and passion for the topic; and,
- set the moral tone for subsequent discussions.

The lecture is a useful format by which to transmit information. However, it must convey far more than what can be gained by reading the written word. The primary difference between reading a book and listening to a lecture is that there is a person present in the lecture. A videotape of a person talking adds a human and visual dimension, but provides no opening for interaction or flexibility. Although in each of these cases the main communication is from educator to students, opportunities exist in a live lecture for interaction, questioning, illustration, elaboration, explanation, inclusion of personal anecdotes, humor, expressiveness, enthusiasm, movement, and change of pace. The lecture method should be used when these characteristics are important; otherwise, reading transmits information just as effectively, and class time can be used in a different way.

Demonstrations by an instructor or on a screen are intended to show students how to carry out a procedure or task. A videotape, or even a series of drawings, can accomplish this; these methods are simple to use, easy for students to view clearly, cheap, and reusable. However, a live demonstration by the instructor adds several dimensions to the learning experience—the chance for students to interrupt and ask questions, the addition of input from senses other than sight and sound, the possibility of elaboration, the use of humor and personal anecdotes for emphasis, and, in some cases, the opportunity to be in a specific setting such as a shop or hospital.

Giving Inspirational Lectures and Demonstrations

As discussed in Chapter Three, faculty have different personalities and preferences. We cannot all aspire to be charismatic and dynamic lecturers, holding audiences of several hundred students spellbound for three hours a week. It is important to be authentic, true to oneself, and work with, not against, one's personality. Given that caveat, there are ways to make lectures and demonstrations stimulating, involving, and inspirational. Following are some of Brookfield's (1990) guidelines on creative lecturing and Wlodkowski's (1990) strategies for maintaining learner attention.

Given that our attention span for listening is between twelve and twenty minutes, the *pace* of a lecture is important. Brookfield suggests breaking up a lecture by asking questions, providing opportunities for students to ask questions, having students discuss an issue with a neighbor, initiating stretch breaks, or providing time to review notes silently. These techniques can be used in a class of any size as long as the lecturer is willing to tolerate the resulting noise or potential confusion.

Both lectures and demonstrations can be *personalized.* Faculty can draw on their own experiences, introduce issues they have thought or read about, tell amusing anecdotes, or illustrate points by referring to current events, books, television programs, or films. These techniques allow the educator to be an accessible and real person, and therefore much more interesting than a remote and impersonal lecturer or a "talking head" at the front of the hall who might just as well be on videotape. Students come to appreciate and enjoy the personal characteristics or quirks of their teacher when that teacher is an actual person to them. This, in turn, can lead students to approach the content of their course with a more positive, enthusiastic attitude as interest in the teacher sparks interest in the field.

In the same way, it is important to be *spontaneous* rather than stilted. Preparing a written text for a lecture or demonstration and reading that text, or, even worse, reading excerpts from a textbook, seems artificial and quickly becomes boring. Written text and natural speech use different words, style, rhythms, and intonation. Unless one is reading poetry or dramatic passages from literature, reading provides a poor basis for a lecture and has a negative effect on students. For example, I received a message from a friend telling me that her daughter spent the weekend in tears after her first week of university classes. Her professors, she said, all read, and read poorly, to the class. She had been excited about attending university and now could see no purpose in attending the lectures.

However, Brookfield (1990) emphasizes that unplanned talking is not a good alternative to reading from a text and suggests that organized notes be used to guide the flow of the lecture. Some instructors jot points on index cards, some use text on overhead transparencies as a guide, others have their preparatory notes, still others keep a written lecture in front of them, but only use it as a guide. Without structure and reminders, lectures can lose focus, skip important information, proceed illogically, and ultimately confuse the listener.

Visual aids enhance any presentation. They give students something else to look at, serve as a focus for points that are being made in speech, provide an explicit organization and structure, illustrate points through drawings or photographs, and add humor. If some students are primarily visual learners and others primarily auditory learners, using visual aids in addition to a lecture addresses both ways of learning. Visual aids include overhead transparencies, posted flip chart paper, computer generated graphics projected onto a screen, videotapes, or chalkboards and whiteboards. The message may include a quotation from a famous author, an outline of the main points in the presentation, a pictorial representation of a concept, a figure or chart, or a cartoon or joke.

Brookfield (1990) suggests that a lecture should end with a *question*. Rather than ending with a summary, he encourages instructors to pose a question that is critical to the lecture itself, a question about unresolved issues raised by the content or about future directions that may emerge. I would add that questions also can be used to introduce a lecture or demonstration, focus or refocus during a session, and encourage student involvement. Questions should be interesting and provocative, not focusing on factual material, but instead asking learners to make connections among ideas, analyze or challenge what has been said, and relate material to personal experience.

Variety in personal style is recommended by Wlodkowski (1990) as a way of engaging learners' attention in a lecture or demonstration. He suggests five presentation characteristics that can be varied to maintain interest.

- Some body movement is desirable—walking across the room, along the sides, among the students. Body language can express enthusiasm and animation.

- Smiling, using gestures, and changing facial expression adds variety to a presentation.
- Variation in one's voice is critical. Interest is enhanced by using different tones and pitches, as well as using the voice to convey emphasis, emotion, and support.
- Pauses are essential—they break up the flow of the information, create a contrast, emphasize a point, and allow a moment for reflection.
- Finally, eye contact indicates an interest in the learners and their response to the presentation. Even in a large group, it is possible to look directly at individuals. However, prolonged eye contact can make people uncomfortable.

The use of *humor, metaphor, and stories* brightens up a demonstration or lecture. Humor should be natural and spontaneous, so if it does not come easily, it should not be attempted. Still, most of us can tell a relevant joke from the morning newspaper. People like to laugh, and when the teacher is trying to be funny, students almost always enjoy it. Metaphor often encourages learners to look at a concept from a different perspective—they are novel and therefore interesting. A well-told story can enchant a class, as well as provide an unusual way of making a point.

Wlodkowski (1990) recommends both *unpredictability* and *disequilibrium* as techniques to make demonstrations or lectures stimulating and involving, cautioning us that learners need to feel secure before such strategies are used. As examples of unpredictability, he suggests lecturing from a seat in the classroom, acting slightly out of character, or telling a self-deprecating story. Creating disequilibrium can be done by presenting contradictions or disturbing data and information, playing the devil's advocate, or breaking off the class in the middle of an interesting point.

Finally, actually *seeing oneself* give a demonstration or a lecture is an invaluable experience. Have someone videotape a session, then review that videotape, focusing on the points raised here and any others that emerge from the tape. This is an extremely effective technique to improve our presentations. In this way we actually see ourselves as our students see us—voice, mannerisms, body language, pacing of the session, questioning techniques, and spontaneity. Although it sounds intimidating, every faculty member I have worked with, after overcoming initial anxiety, has valued the experience. The videotape should be watched privately first; then it may be watched with a trusted colleague or an instructional developer to give another perspective—but this second step is not as important as the first.

Problem-Based Learning

In problem-based learning, students encounter the principles, concepts, theories, and ideas of a subject in the context of solving a problem (Barrows and Tamblyn, 1980). The learning may be individual or collaborative. The problems are presented in a variety of formats in different subjects. These may be as complex as medical diagnoses of actual or simulated patients, statistical analyses of data sets, the construction of a wood frame building, and the development of software, or as straightforward as solving basic mathematics and science problems. What distinguishes problem-based learning from more instructor-centered approaches is that students acquire theoretical and factual information through working on a concrete problem. When theory is needed to solve the problem, students find out about the theory. In contrast, lectures and demonstrations first impart information, which is then applied to problems. For example, after students attend a lecture, they follow it by seeing how the concepts work in practice in the laboratory.

Why use a problem-based learning approach in the transmission of instrumental knowledge and technical skills? Problem-based learning leads to the acquisition of the relevant cognitive skills and also may develop interpersonal skills if the problems are worked on collaboratively by students. It clearly increases students' active involvement in the learning process. Problem-based learning becomes more difficult to implement when the class is large, but it can be done. Gilbert (1995) makes a provocative argument for the irrelevance of class size—among other strategies that he suggests for active learning in large classes is problem-based learning.

Since problem-based learning clearly requires more preparation time and is more difficult to manage than a lecture or a demonstration, when should it be used? When is the extra time and trouble worthwhile? This issue returns us to the questions posed in Chapter Four: What is the rationale for the curriculum? What is the purpose of the class? If the expectation is that students will be able to solve problems when they have finished the class, course, or program, then it is a good idea to involve them in solving problems during their learning experience. At this juncture, there are two choices. We can provide theoretical concepts, principles, or formulae in a lecture and ask students to work out problems at home. Or, we can center and build the course on problems, with theoretical points emerging as needed.

There is no one right choice. However, the more central problem solving is to the subject being taught, the more appropriate is problem-based learning. In medical education, for example, where problem-based learning is commonly used, the ability to solve clinical problems is of primary importance. For a virtual reality course in a computer applications program, the ability to work with rapidly changing technology is critical to student success; current theory is less important as it is constantly becoming outdated and revised. Faculty who are considering the use of problem-based learning must decide whether problem solving is central to their course. If so, that decision must be weighed against such constraints as time, resource availability, and class size. The importance of student involvement in the learning process must also be acknowledged. We know that increasing involvement facilitates learning for most students, and problem-based learning is an ideal way to boost involvement.

Designing Effective Problem-Based Learning

The problems developed for problem-based learning must be *meaningful*. If students can simply look up solutions in a textbook, little learning will occur. Solving problems should require research and reading, analysis of the task, synthesis of ideas, generation of alternatives, questioning of alternatives, and finally the selection of the best solution.

Designing meaningful problems is time consuming, but well worth the effort. If learners can also be involved in problem conception, their involvement and sense of responsibility is further enhanced—this involvement is possible in upper level courses and with smaller groups.

The problems should be not only meaningful, but *interesting* to the learners. By drawing on the experience and background of learners, building in current issues or controversies, relating the problems to the workplace, arranging that the gathering of data occurs outside the classroom, and making the applications clear, problems can be created that are motivating and interesting to work on.

Directions and expectations should be clear. At first glance, the use of general or vaguely defined problems may seem to add complexity, but it is more likely to frustrate students and lead to unsuccessful or unintended results. The level of specificity of the directions should take into account the prior knowledge and expertise of the learners. The more advanced the students are, the less detail is required. But, in all cases, expectations must be clear. If at all possible, students should be involved in developing these expectations. In some cases, this can be a part of the problem itself. Students, with the educator acting as facilitator, can decide what format the results should take, or what the product should look like.

Since the goal of problem-based learning is that students gain theoretical knowledge through the activities, the problems need to be designed in such a way that they *unveil theoretical concepts*. The solution to the problems should lead the students to discover and become familiar with the major concepts and principles of the course. In order to ensure that this happens, the instructor can list or draw a conceptual map of all of the theoretical points to be conveyed and create one or more problems to deal with each point. In a college course on refrigeration, for example, if it is considered important that learners become familiar with the relationship between the characteristics of freon and its effect on the earth's ozone layer, a problem should be included to lead students to investigate this issue.

Problem-based learning is most effective if the solution of the problem calls for *interaction* among learners. In this way, involvement is further increased and students gain skills related to working in teams. For example, students can be encouraged to break a problem up into parts, with two people investigating each part and bringing the information back to the group. Brainstorming techniques can be effective. Achieving consensus on the best solution then becomes a part of the process. Continued discussion can be the primary method of working on the problem.

The educator should be open to and available for *consultation* during problem-based learning. Teachers can not go off and work on personal research projects once the students are occupied elsewhere. It is a good idea to build consultation meetings with individuals or groups into the process, be present on a regular basis when students are working in their groups, bring resources and ideas into the groups, and generally stay closely involved in the learning process.

Care needs to be taken that *fair evaluation* procedures are used, especially when students are working collaboratively on the problems. We all are familiar with the situation in which one member of a group project is accused of not doing his or her fair share of the work and yet receives the same evaluation as the others. Such difficulties can undermine the effectiveness of problem-based learning and give it a bad reputation, especially among hard-working students. Individual or group self-evaluation can help. Clear criteria for evaluation are critical. Open and frank discussions about evaluation before any dilemmas develop are important.

Experiential Learning

Experiential learning has long been advocated in public school and adult education. It is based on the belief as expressed by Dewey (1938, p. 25) that "all genuine education comes about through experience." In higher education, experiential learning is commonly found in professional schools (e.g., teacher training practica and nursing students' clinical experiences), in the trades and technologies (e.g., shop work and apprenticeships), and in science (e.g., laboratory experiences). Recently, experiential learning has become even more important with the popular advent and inclusion of assessments of prior learning. In the United States, over 1000 colleges allow students to obtain college credits for demonstrating relevant, prior experiential learning (McCormick, 1990). Cooperative education, in which students alternate periods of full-time study with periods of full-time employment, is another version of experiential learning. Experiential learning can take place in the classroom through simulations, games, role plays, and the like. Lee and Caffarella (1994) list 16 techniques for engaging learners in experiential learning in in-class activities. Many of their suggestions are more appropriate for communicative than instrumental learning; nevertheless it is important for us to consider the possibility of introducing experiential learning in the classroom in any situation.

Why choose experiential learning for the acquisition of instrumental knowledge and technical skills? According to Kolb (1984), true learning occurs only when learners have concrete experiences, reflect on these experiences, create generalizations or principles that integrate their observations, and then test out what they have learned in more complex situations. Kolb is only one of many theorists who argue that experience is essential to learning. We can listen and read, but what we learn is not meaningful until it is put into practice or experienced. However, according to psychological type theory (Chapter Three), not all individuals prefer to learn in this way.

It needs to be very clear that experiential learning is valid not only for the acquisition of instrumental knowledge and technical skills. Experiential learning is relevant for all domains of knowledge (see, for example, Kolb's (1984) work and Jackson and Caffarella's (1994) collection of essays). In Chapters Six and Seven, many of the strategies for facilitating communicative knowledge and fostering emancipatory learning are experiential in nature. I include experiential learning as a primary strategy in this chapter so as to encourage faculty to think about what they may already be doing from a new perspective, as well as to suggest that experiential methods be used to supplement lectures and demonstrations whenever relevant and possible.

Experiential learning should be used whenever students need to learn to perform actual skills—for example, operate forestry equipment, give medication, take x-rays, repair a small engine, or pronounce words in a second language. Any time the acquisition of a technical skill is a goal of a course, it is essential that the learning is experiential. Reading a manual or watching a demonstration may set the stage for learning, but cannot take the place of performance.

Experiential learning also is appropriate when the application of instrumental knowledge in a real setting is important. Students in a hospitality program at a college may learn about the functioning of a hotel or a tourist information program in the classroom, but it is only when they spend time in the actual workplace that this information becomes truly meaningful. In many such programs, educators often find little relationship between how well students do in the classroom and how well they do in the work setting, as transfer of learning from one setting to another is by no means automatic. The acquisition of knowledge and applying it successfully in a real-life situation are two different things; when application of what has been learned is the goal, it needs to be experienced.

When the synthesis of knowledge is important, but field experiences are out of the question because they are too costly or time-consuming, in-class experiential learning activities are an option. Lee and Caffarella (1994) state that such techniques also increase learner responsibility or self-direction and enhance knowledge richness. Again, transfer of knowledge to the real-life situation is not guaranteed. In-class activities may include, for example, a simulation of responding to work orders, the repair of a model of a computer, a case study of why the electrical system on a ship failed, or a role play of a nursing diagnosis. The specific nature of the techniques used depends on the subject.

Planning Meaningful Experiential Learning Activities

In this section, I draw in part on suggestions made by Lee and Caffarella (1994). They discuss ways in which experiential learning activities may be enhanced so as to increase knowledge synthesis, self-directed learning, and knowledge richness.

When planning experiential learning activities in the field, *site selection* must be done with care. The site should have up-to-date equipment and resources, the staff should be knowledgeable and interested in having students present, the procedures used on the site should be congruent with the procedures being taught in the classroom, and the site should be accessible to students and the educator. The instructor should visit the site more than once and talk to as many staff as possible before making the selection. I have heard more than one story of staff on the site undermining the educator's work by showing students unsafe short cuts and even unethical practices.

It may be advisable to include *more than one site* in order to expose students to different situations and contrasting points of view in their field. For example, large and small organizations or public and private institutions have varying climates, cultures, and work policies. Giving students experience on different sites enriches their learning and also may help them decide which kind of organization they want to work with upon graduation.

Kolb (1984) describes four *types of learning environments,* each of which is important for a different learning skill or mode.

- *Affectively complex environments* are ones in which the emphasis is on learning what it is actually like to be a professional in the field.
- *Perceptually complex environments* are ones in which the goal is to collect information, gain different perspectives, and understand a process.
- *Symbolically complex environments* are ones in which the learner solves abstract problems for which there are right answers.
- Finally, *behaviorally complex environments* are those in which the emphasis is on completing practical tasks.

It is important to choose the type of site for experiential learning which best matches the goals of the program or course.

Educators should ensure that the experiential learning activity has *depth* and *comprehensiveness.* Usually, we want students to be exposed to as many facets of the field as possible. We want their experience to have depth as well as breadth. That is, students should have an opportunity to participate in complex procedures, be involved in innovative projects, and attend staff meetings. On some sites, students are taken advantage of and assigned menial or routine tasks to complete. The learning experience of one mechanic apprentice consisted primarily of cleaning the shop floor and keeping the tools in order. Visiting the sites regularly and keeping in close contact with students helps prevent such incidents.

Experiential learning can be reinforced through the use of *journals* or *logbooks,* which stimulate reflection on the experience and encourage synthesis of what is learned. Journals or logbooks may take many different forms (see Chapter Seven). In nursing, students commonly divide each page of their log in half vertically, recording on one side of the page what they actually did in their clinical experience, and on the other side listing their questions, thoughts, or feelings about the experience. Arranging for students to have an on-site *mentor* helps make the experiential learning more meaningful. A mentor introduces the learner to the procedures and routines of the organization, provides support, answers questions, and generally is available to help out when things are confusing, overwhelming, or frustrating. In teacher training, for example, students work closely with an associate teacher, a person who guides them through their initial experiences in the classroom and gradually turns over more responsibility as confidence and skill grow. This model can be applied to any setting, although it may not always be practical because of the time required of the mentor.

Experiential learning requires *debriefing* through discussion, either when students are back in the classroom or at the end of the day or week on the site. Students have the chance to recount their experiences, obtain advice from the teacher and fellow students, and present questions or issues arising from the experience. In many nursing programs, for example, a clinical conference is held at the end of the day—students and teacher meet in small groups to discuss the events they have weathered. This is often the time when learners realize that they were not the only ones who were confused or lost, and made mistakes. It is also a time when the educator can critically question learners about their experiences. Support and challenge need to be carefully balanced as always.

An alternative to debriefing is to require a *written follow-up* or report at the end of an experiential learning activity. The educator can respond to the report in writing, ask questions about the experience, and perhaps incorporate the report into the course evaluation. However, a written follow-up is not as effective as discussion since learners do not share their experiences with each other and receive the peer support that comes from a group.

Lee and Caffarella (1994) recommend that educators encourage *long-term networking* to be developed out of experiential learning. In addition to staying in touch with their peers, students can establish staff contacts who may provide support after entry into the workforce. Transfer and reinforcement of learning is furthered when networking continues after program completion. Students can also establish contacts and stay in touch with future potential employers.

When experiential learning activities are carried out in the classroom, every attempt should be made to ensure that the experiences are as *realistic* and *authentic* as possible. When role plays or simulations are used, take the time to set up a few props and establish an atmosphere that resembles the real setting. Actual case studies from the field are more realistic than textbook cases. For example, one college instructor in marine mechanics, with access to and permission to use shipping accident files, presented the first part of the report to his students, handing out the end of the file—what actually happened—after students had worked on the case.

For in-class activities, working in *teams* or *groups* is recommended rather than independent or competitive exercises. Students benefit from the added interaction and involvement possible in a small group. This approach serves to enhance learning, as well as improve interpersonal skills, and resembles the workplace where most organizations now advocate team work.

Critical Thinking

One common and serious problem in conveying instrumental knowledge and technical skills is the extent to which that knowledge may go unquestioned. We are used to criticizing political systems or psychological theories, but are much less likely to question information that is presented as and assumed to be objective or scientifically correct. Yet, what was objective and scientifically proven ten years, or even one year ago, may no longer be considered to be so today. For this reason, faculty must encourage their students to engage in critical thinking in the instrumental domain of knowledge.

Habermas (1971) criticizes the manner in which the processes of rational thought are applied to all spheres of knowledge. He distinguishes between cause and effect relationships that will always be true, in all situations, such as laws of gravity, and those that may change due to various conditions or social factors. When a statement is true in the empirical sciences, it must stand up to scientific discourse—the collection and examination of evidence. This is the foundation of critical thinking. Our students should not, then, merely listen to us lecture, read texts, take notes, and accept what they hear and read. Instead, they should actively engage in the kind of thought that leads to instrumental knowledge, including questioning what they hear and read.

Although there are many different models of critical thinking, including Paul's (1990) comprehensive works and King and Kitchener's (1994) developmental approach, I present Brookfield's (1987, 1995) practical and straightforward guidelines for questioning what we hear and see. He outlines four components central to critical thinking.

- We need to identify the assumptions that underlie the ideas we normally take for granted and ask questions about the accuracy and validity of those assumptions.
- We need to be aware of and challenge the influence of our context on what we believe to be true.
- We need to imagine and explore alternatives to our existing ways of thinking.

- We need to be reflectively skeptical—because everyone believes something or because an authority figure has told us that this is so, this need not make it so.

Encouraging Critical Thinking

Encouraging critical thinking is not an activity or a technique that can be tacked on to an already prepared course or lecture series. It is a way of being as a teacher that is integrated throughout one's practice. I do suggest some specific techniques for stimulating critical thought, but it is more important that an underlying attitude of reflective skepticism permeate the teaching and learning process.

Modeling critical thinking as we teach is perhaps the most important thing we can do. Brookfield (1987, 1995) describes how we can model risk taking, assumption analysis, and openness. By risk taking he means taking a gamble with the teaching process itself—trying something new, departing from the agenda, or experimenting with an alternative viewpoint. Being explicit about taking risks shows students that it is acceptable and even fun to step away from accepted routine. Questioning or analyzing one's own assumptions about the subject or teaching process validates this process for students. Stopping to say, "I've always believed this, but I wonder, is it necessarily true?" in the middle of an explanation can have a profound effect, especially when students often regard their instructor as an expert, and one beyond question. Openness about doubts, questions, and uncertainties indicates to students that this is a positive and productive undertaking.

Encouraging students to engage in *critical questioning* is a key part of critical thinking. As described in Chapter One, three kinds of questions lead to different levels of reflection: content, process, and premise. We question the content of an experience by asking "What happened?" or the process by asking "How did things come to be the way they are?" Questioning the underlying premise is most likely to lead to critical reflection. By asking "Why does this matter in the first place?" we focus on the basic assumptions upon which the content rests. Faculty can ask critical questions of both their students and themselves. Most importantly, they should invite learners to ask critical questions about the subject and the course.

Although it is questioned whether critical thinking can be taught separately from content, some teaching techniques are likely to stimulate critical thinking. Among other methods, Brookfield (1987) suggests the use of *debates, brainstorming,* and *critical incidents.* Such strategies can be most useful within the context of the discipline. Choosing an issue from the course outline and setting up a *debate,* either formal or informal, encourages students to see things from at least two perspectives. It is interesting to ask students to argue for a point of view that is contrary to the one they hold as this is more likely to stimulate critical thinking than arguing for a familiar position. *Brainstorming* is an activity in which learners generate as many alternative ideas as possible without judging the quality of the ideas. Outrageous and silly suggestions are fine and, in fact, may either contain or lead to creative ideas. This quick technique can be used on many topics and in a class of any size. Generating alternatives leads us to question the way things are. The technique of *critical incidents* asks students to describe either the best scenario they have experienced or the worst. In a professional program, for example, following a field experience, the educator could ask students to relate their best moment or their worst moment (or both). Discussion of the incident focuses on the underlying assumptions: What made it a good moment? Why is that important to you? This, in turn, can lead to critical thinking.

Brookfield (1987) proposes several strategies for developing alternative ways of thinking. Among them are variations on the theme of *imagining the future*. In any discipline, one can ask students to speculate on how knowledge will develop in the future, leading directly to critical thinking about how things are now. Learners can imagine that it is five years in the future and describe what they see. They can develop preferred scenarios by considering questions such as, "What would this problem look like if it were managed differently?" (Brookfield, 1987, p. 120). Such activities can form part of a discussion or be presented as exercises for group work. One must be cautious about using future-oriented assignments for individual students. As I discussed in Chapter Three, individuals with a preference for the sensing psychological function over the intuitive are grounded in the present and are not comfortable with these activities. In a small group, they are stimulated by the discussion, but if they are working independently, frustration rather than critical thinking may be the result.

Summary

One of the three broad goals of higher education is the transmittal of instrumental knowledge and technical skills on which society will always depend. Rapid changes in the nature of knowledge make it essential that we do not expect our students to memorize facts, but instead teach in ways that lead them to be lifelong learners.

Lectures and demonstrations, the most common teaching strategies in colleges and universities, are an effective way of transmitting instrumental knowledge and technical skills. A good lecture or demonstration utilizes the personal element. It is after all, a real person that makes the difference between a lecture and a videotape or a textbook. Demonstrations and lectures can be inspiring, spontaneous, humorous, creative, and fun to participate in.

Problem-based learning allows students to acquire theoretical concepts through the process of solving problems or doing tasks. It is one way of encouraging the kind of lifelong learning skills that our students now need. Effective problem-based learning presents students with meaningful and interesting tasks and is designed in such a way that the relevant theory must be learned in order to solve the problem. Ideally, problem-based learning also involves interaction, collaboration, and consultation.

Although experiential learning is by no means useful only in the domain of instrumental knowledge, it is a natural approach when students are learning to perform skills or to apply knowledge in actual settings. The selection of the field site is important in planning good experiential learning activities, as is good follow-up in the form of journals, discussions, or reports. Experiential learning activities can also be designed for the classroom; making them as realistic as possible is important.

All instrumental knowledge must be open to scrutiny. Critical thinking is a commonly espoused goal of higher education, but it is less noticeable in practice. As educators, we need to model critical thinking ourselves by taking risks, questioning our own assumptions, and being open to alternative views. At the same time, we should actively encourage critical thinking among our learners.

Chapter Six

Facilitating Communicative Knowledge

Our deep-rooted need to understand each other and be understood has inspired thinkers and writers throughout history. Although, at one time, science and its methods were expected to provide all answers to our social problems, this hope is gradually fading. We only need consider attempting to isolate and quantify all of the variables in a single classroom in order to scientifically investigate the teaching and learning process to see that this is an impossible endeavor. To understand a culture or a political system in this way is even more difficult to envision. Thus, more researchers, writers, and thinkers are now turning to interpretive strategies in order to understand the nature of society and its citizens.

Communicative knowledge, or practical knowledge as Habermas (1971) calls it, is subjectively derived through language. In other words, through interaction with others we build and gain knowledge of our social norms, values, ideals, political and educational systems, and culture. Unlike instrumental knowledge, this kind of awareness does not result in ability to predict and control, but leads instead to an intersubjective understanding. The goal is to understand what others mean and to make ourselves understood, both on an individual and a social level. Communicative knowledge is not prescriptive—it does not lead to solutions to problems, nor formulae that govern behavior.

When all people in a group agree on a value, norm, or way of doing things, they have constructed communicative knowledge. The group may be a classroom, an organization, a community, a country, or a culture. Since coming to consensus through discussion is central to communicative knowledge, the way in which it takes place is critical. Manipulation of people's views through the media or empty political rhetoric distorts knowledge. Mezirow (1991, pp. 77-78) outlines the optimal conditions for participation in discourse. People will:

- have accurate and complete information;
- be free from coercion and distorting self-deception;
- weigh evidence and assess arguments;
- be open to alternative perspectives;
- critically reflect on presuppositions;
- have equal opportunity to participate; and,
- accept informed consensus as valid knowledge.

Most faculty would agree that these characteristics comprise ideal conditions for participation in learning in our classrooms—not that all of these conditions are ever in place, but this is what we hope and strive for.

As I mention in Chapter One, knowledge of teaching is, in itself, communicative knowledge. In addition, much of what we want our students in higher education to acquire is communicative knowledge. The social sciences, professional schools, and arts and humanities are to a large extent about understanding ourselves, others, and our social worlds. In areas where we work to meet the needs of business and industry, the emphasis is increasingly placed on interpersonal abilities, emotional intelligence, and generic work skills.

In this chapter, I review four sets of strategies for facilitating communicative knowledge in colleges and universities. The process of discussion is emphasized first as it is central to all communicative learning processes. I then consider how collaborative learning takes place through group work, role plays, and case studies, and finally examine the importance of networks and support groups. For each, I provide suggestions as to when to use the strategy and ideas on how to enhance the quality of the process.

Discussion

Since communicative knowledge is developed through language, all communicative learning must be based on interaction with others. The term, "discourse," is often used in the literature on communicative learning. In ordinary dialogue or discussion, we describe experiences and express opinions. However, in discourse, questions of truth, justice, and accurate perception are raised: the central process is the challenging of common beliefs.

Nevertheless, I use the term, "discussion," here, as it is more familiar to teachers. The ideal conditions of discourse, however, should be kept in mind as a part of our understanding of discussion that has learning as its goal.

When should we use discussion? Almost every chance we get when communicative learning is our goal. Given this overall guideline, we must be very clear about why we are using discussion in a course. The rationale behind our strategies always needs to be articulated. Brookfield (1990, pp. 93-96) lists several purposes of discussion, all of which fall into the communicative domain of learning:

- to explore a diversity of perspectives;
- to assist students in discovering new perspectives;
- to emphasize the complexity and ambiguity of issues;
- to help students recognize their own assumptions;
- to increase students' ability to defend their ideas;
- to encourage careful listening to others;
- to increase students' sense of involvement with the topic;
- to show students that their experiences are valued;

- to help develop a sense of group identity; and,
- to encourage democratic habits.

To encourage optimal conditions for discourse, I add further points to this list:

- to gather information through others' experiences;
- to learn respect for others' viewpoints;
- to display how to weigh evidence and assess arguments;
- to demonstrate the process of reaching consensus; and,
- to develop the ability to contribute to discussions.

Whenever a few or several of these purposes are a part of a curriculum rationale, discussion is an appropriate strategy. As meaningful discussion is not possible without accurate and complete information, readings, presentations of different viewpoints, or experiences in the field must precede sessions.

Facilitating Meaningful Discussions

Most of us have experienced poor discussions—where we were excruciatingly bored, too intimidated to speak, frustrated by someone with nothing of interest to say who monopolized the period, or baffled by seemingly off-topic digressions. How can we ensure that discussions fulfill the purposes for which we intend them? Since discussion involves complex group dynamics, what will happen is not predictable. Too much control by educators defeats the purpose of discussion, yet we have a responsibility to make the process interesting, informative, and worthwhile. Some of the following guidelines are adapted from Brookfield's (1990) suggestions.

The *purpose* of a discussion should be made explicit to the group. If the aim is to explore alternative points of view, learners need to know this so that they feel free to explore possibilities, rather than attempt to come up with the right or best solution. If the purpose relates to group dynamics, that is, to further understanding and cohesion among the members of the group, then this must be clear so that students do not see the discussion as a waste of time or irrelevant to the topic. Having a hidden agenda never works. Students sense that they are being manipulated and try to uncover the teacher's real motives.

Similarly, the instructor should not *secretly plan* that the discussion result in a specific conclusion or outcome. Many of us have witnessed this approach to leading a discussion. Some points are ignored, others emphasized, and strategically placed summaries on the part of the leader bring the group to the intended end result. This reflects the educator's belief that his or her view is the correct one, and therefore defeats the purpose of discussion—engaging in collaborative inquiry where each participant's contribution is equally valid.

We need to ensure that students are *informed* and *prepared* for a discussion. This may involve providing the discussion question in a previous class and suggesting readings or other preparatory activities. Alternatively, material can be presented in the form of a videotape, handouts, or oral presentation just prior to the discussion. Informed students are less likely to relate irrelevant experiences or wander off topic. The instructor needs to be equally informed and prepared, while remaining open to the directions the discussion may take.

The discussion topics or questions need to be *interesting* and *relevant* to the students. A controversial topic naturally engenders more discussion than one on which everyone agrees. However, a topic that the instructor considers controversial is not always regarded as such by a class, so alternative discussion questions may be prepared in case some are not of interest. If the topics can be personalized or made relevant to students' actual experiences, increased involvement is likely. On the other hand, some learners are, by nature, more interested in abstract, theoretical questions or future-oriented issues while others are more inclined to discuss practical, down-to-earth topics (see Chapter Three). If this is the case, sub-groups of a class may elect to discuss different aspects of the same topic. This strategy allows everyone to be involved in a way that is meaningful to them. If the small groups share what they talked about with the whole class, no one misses the main points of any aspect of the discussion.

The *environment* of the classroom can be made conducive to discussion. When possible, the physical environment should be arranged so that everyone can see everyone else and no positions, including that of the teacher, imply dominance. In other words, no "teacher's desk" or podium should be in sight; the instructor sits with the group. A circle is usually best, but not feasible if the group is larger. Brookfield (1995) notes that the circular arrangement can be intimidating for some students. Groups of tables can break a larger group into smaller discussion groups. Carpets, good lighting, and a pleasant room all help. In small seminars, encouraging students to take turns bringing refreshments can change the environment—the smell of fresh coffee or the sight of a plate of cookies lightens everyone's mood. Admittedly, sometimes, we can do nothing about the classroom environment. In those cases, we need to rely on encouraging a positive atmosphere and attitude.

The *atmosphere* in the classroom should encourage everyone to participate or feel that they have an equal opportunity to participate. This is less tangible than setting up the physical environment and more difficult to achieve. Discussion in groups sometimes takes on a life of its own very early on in a course—a pattern which can be hard to change. The teacher can model acceptance of everyone's contribution. Keeping quiet and encouraging participants to speak to each other rather than through the teacher helps. The teacher who presents himself or herself as a person—approachable, enthusiastic, authentic, and concerned—also contributes to an atmosphere in which students feel free to participate.

It is important to remember that no one should feel compelled to speak. More introverted students feel uncomfortable in an atmosphere where they are expected to participate even when they have nothing to say. Knox (1986) suggests the use of informal warm-up activities, games, icebreakers, and puzzles as a way of encouraging everyone to feel part of a group. Also, breaking a class into smaller discussion groups of four or five individuals tends to give even the quietest of learners a chance to talk.

It is equally important that no one or two people dominate discussion, making it difficult for others to contribute. Sometimes, it is appropriate for the class to set up its own rules for discussion and take responsibility for reminding each other when violations occur. At other times, it is appropriate for the educator to intervene gently in the discussion and ask someone else to offer their view. If neither of these approaches work, a third strategy may be to speak privately to over-eager contributors. Often people do not have a realistic sense of the amount or nature of what they say to the group. For example, in an attempt to curtail an aggressive student, I once made a comment in a group feedback session that one or two people dominated the discussion. Even the most reticent of group members confessed that they thought I was speaking about them.

These strategies are primarily focused on supporting discussion. Equally important to meaningful discourse, is *challenging* learners' points of view. If it is the practice in the class that ideas and comments are questioned by others, both teacher and learners, more significant learning takes place than if all contributions are routinely accepted. In Chapter Four, I mention the importance of balancing support and challenge, and I reiterate that point here. To challenge each other may be uncomfortable, initially, in a learning group. People prefer to be kind to others and may see challenges as aggressive acts. However, if we see this in relation to one of the optimal conditions for participation in discourse—that people will be able to weigh evidence and assess arguments—challenge can become a natural part of the conversation. Challenging points in a discussion then becomes a matter of asking participants for evidence for their statements or arguing for an alternative viewpoint in a logical, reasonable way. The content, process, and premise reflection questions can provide a framework: What is your viewpoint? How did you come to hold that view (or, what is your evidence)? Why is this important to the discussion? For students to be comfortable with their teacher challenging their views, they need to trust him or her, and this takes time to establish.

Some learners are more reluctant to challenge their peers than others. People with a preference for the psychological type function of feeling, for example, may see this process as producing conflict, a state of affairs they do not enjoy. Other learners may find it difficult to argue for an alternative viewpoint in a logical fashion. It is important that we realize and allow for these differences among students. Small group discussion may help learners feel more comfortable. Also, once everyone becomes accustomed to being challenged and challenging others, much of the unease wears off.

Reviewing or *summarizing* a discussion helps learners to go over the main points in their minds; however, as Brookfield (1990) points out, a definitive summary provided by the teacher goes against the open-ended, pluralistic nature of good discourse. It sets up the expectation that there is a right answer, and now that the discussion is over, the teacher will supply it. This is exactly what we do not want students to expect at the end of a discussion. One alternative is to ask students to summarize the discussion; another is to ask students to present unanswered questions that have arisen out of the discussion (Brookfield, 1990). Many times, I have been astonished when a student comes up with a summary as definitive as the kind we have been warned against, and also one that seems to me to be barely related to the discussion I thought I heard. Asking for two different summaries may help. Summarizing through questions may be the more useful suggestion.

Collaborative Learning through Group Work

Group work may take place within a class in small group discussions, or outside the classroom as students work on projects or participate in field experiences together. In-class activities usually last only a short time, although it is possible to have students work in the same small group throughout a course. Group work often lasts longer when it occurs outside the classroom, though some special events may only be a day or half-day long.

When is group work collaborative? The term "collaborative" has come to have a special meaning in education, even though the dictionary simply defines it as "working together." In the literature, collaborative learning is defined as shared inquiry. Learners work together to construct knowledge rather than to discover objective truths (for example, see Cranton, 1996b). It is therefore distinguished from cooperative learning, a structured process in which students work together to solve a problem or complete an assigned task.

Cooperative learning is considered useful for acquiring instrumental knowledge whereas collaborative learning is more suitable for building communicative knowledge. Imel (1991) lists five bases for collaborative learning.

- Both facilitators and learners are active participants.
- The hierarchy between teachers and learners is eliminated.
- A sense of community is created.
- Knowledge is created, not transferred.
- Knowledge is seen to be located in the community.

When is collaborative group work appropriate? Clearly, facilitating communicative knowledge is collaborative in nature. As collaborative learning has developed as an educational practice, it has become tied to the concept of constructed or communicative knowledge. In collaborative learning groups diverse student experiences, ideas, values, and insights can be brought together in order to try and understand the nature of human interactions (Cranton, 1996b). Here, learners are more likely to gain meaningful new perspectives and ideas than they can by absorbing one expert view. Process and content are inseparable, as opposed to cooperative group learning where the primary focus is on content. Collaborative group work is appropriate in, for example, social sciences, professional schools, management faculties, and training for helping professionals. It is suitable for any learning goal which requires that students bring their ideas together to understand themselves, each other, or the society they live in.

Initiating Constructive Collaborative Group Learning

The educator initiates collaborative group work, but does not thereafter manage or control it. The educator may be a part of the group—Imel's (1991) framework suggests that this is always the case—but he or she is not in charge. The groups have a life of their own, and how the learning proceeds depends primarily on the group rather than on the instructor (which can be difficult for some teachers to accept). I suggest some guidelines to consider in setting up groups, followed by a description of how groups develop over time. In addition, I propose some roles that the educator can adopt during the course of collaborative learning in order to enhance the process.

Ideally, the *composition* of a learning group should be as diverse as possible since collaborative work depends on drawing on a variety of experiences, backgrounds, and areas of expertise. When classes are relatively homogeneous, it is difficult to form diverse small groups. A mixture of learning style or psychological type preferences is also advisable.

Students need some *preparation* to engage in collaborative work. Imel (1991) holds the educator responsible for ensuring that learners understand what collaborative group work entails, as well as its rationale. Learners who are used to individualized, competitive classrooms or teacher-directed approaches may need some time to make the transition to collaborative work.

Whether the group work is of short or long duration, the *nature of the activity* should lead to relevant and meaningful communication among students. The purpose of the activity is to build knowledge and create a new understanding, not to solve a problem that has a pre-determined solution. For example, a group of students in a hospitality course might develop a strategy for improving customer service in a new hotel, or learners in a marketing course might prepare a plan for selling mosquito repellent. There are no right answers to these activities; instead they call on learners to build the knowledge in the group.

Learning group norms need to be established to enable students to work together harmoniously. Does anyone lead the group? Who takes notes? Who is responsible for gathering resources? What will the group do if one individual does not contribute as much as the others? Will individuals in the group have specialized roles? If the group is to meet over several weeks, these issues are more important than if it is a short in-class activity. However, every learning group needs to address some of these issues, even briefly.

The *expectations and outcomes* of group work should be clearly stated and agreed upon by all members. Ideally, the teacher and students work together to develop this framework. A discussion of expectations may address practical issues, such as how long and how often the group will meet, or deal with the nature of the learning goals, such as how deeply the topic will be investigated. Whether the outcome of group work will take the form of a written report, verbal presentation, or practical application needs to be understood by all participants. The general length, quality, and format of the product should be clear.

In collaborative group work, the group members are one important *resource*. Students use their own and each other's experiences and knowledge to build a new understanding. Other resources that students may need—books, materials, access to field sites, experts, and computers—should be made easily available. One responsibility of the educator is to ensure that students will not be frustrated by a lack of resources.

Participation in the *development of a group* is a vital aspect of collaborative learning. In fact, one of the most important benefits of this approach is learning how to work together, including how to handle conflict. Although every group follows its own unique path, a now-classic article by Tuckman (1965) presents a useful general pattern. He suggests five stages of group development.

- In the first, *forming*, group members get to know one another and mutual expectations are shaped.

- The second stage, *storming,* is one in which learners test out their relationships with one another and struggle with individual members' level of commitment.
- In the *norming* stage, group norms, members' roles, and relationships among people are clarified.
- This then allows the *performing* stage to occur, when the work takes place.
- The *adjourning* stage takes place when the group's work is done and people part from each other.

When short-term, in-class group work is carried out, these developmental stages do not occur within small groups, but may still take place in the class as a whole if the class sees itself as a group. In collaborative groups of longer duration, teacher and student awareness of these stages may facilitate the process.

Educator roles may be multi-dimensional. Imel (1991) proposes that in collaborative learning groups, both facilitators and learners are active participants, and the hierarchy of teachers and learners is eliminated. In this case, what is the educator's role? When the educators are participants in learning groups, they become *co-learners.* This is not to say that the teacher's expertise is not recognized by the group, but that the teacher is learning and building understanding along with the group. However, as Brookfield (1995) points out, true equality between teachers and learners is not possible. As *resource* persons, educators contribute materials, readings, and ideas. They also arrange field experiences and access to any additional required resources. When educators participate in collaborative learning, they act as *models* of the process. They demonstrate how to be open to alternative perspectives, engage in critical reflection, and ensure that all have equal opportunity to participate. When problems arise in group work, educators become trouble shooters or *problem solvers.* They arbitrate disputes among group members and help to resolve conflict. Fi-

nally, educators become *advocates* of collaborative learning. For this approach to work, the educator must express
genuine enthusiasm and conviction, which will be conveyed to students and colleagues.

Role Plays and Case Studies

Role plays and case studies are commonly used strategies in the facilitation of communicative learning. Coming
to understand ourselves, others, and the social world we
live in can often be best done through exposure to the
experiences of others. Role plays and case studies allow
us to do this in the classroom—a simulation of real-world
interactions. If students are learning counseling skills, for
example, it is far better that they practice them in role
plays than impose themselves on unsuspecting troubled
clients. By using case studies, students who are acquiring
the understanding necessary to work as managers can do
so with no risk to a real organization.

A role play is a scenario or skit in which learners act
out various parts. It may involve two people, as in the
counseling illustration, or it may involve a group of people
if the scenario is a planning committee, for example. A
role play may be fairly structured, with full information
provided about the various characters in the scenario, or
it may be impromptu and spontaneous. Impromptu role
plays may be introduced on the spur of the moment if an
issue arises in discussion that would benefit from acting
out various parts.

Case studies are written descriptions of a scenario,
situation, or event in which decisions need to be made or
action taken. For example, in an organizational behavior
course, a case study may present a situation in which a
hospital's funding has been cut dramatically and ask
students to consider how the structure of the organization
could be changed to respond to the budget cuts. Like role

plays, case studies either can be structured, with detailed information, or fairly brief, arising on the spot. Generally, case studies based on situations or experiences known to the teacher or the learners are more beneficial than those taken from a textbook. Case studies can be worked on individually, in pairs, or in groups. In fact, they can be projects for a collaborative learning group.

Creating Powerful Role Plays

First, a precautionary note—role playing can be traumatic for some learners. Introverted individuals may find it difficult and embarrassing to perform in front of their peers. Some learners may have had unpleasant experiences in the past with a poorly managed role play and be reluctant to participate. No pressure should be put on people to engage in this strategy if it seriously disturbs them to do so. Role playing is a powerful technique, with the potential for damage if it is not carried out with sensitivity and care.

Role playing can be difficult to use when the class is large. However, if participants are willing to be on stage in front of an audience, it can be effective. Class members who are not designated as players or official observers become the audience.

In giving guidelines for role playing, I draw on some suggestions I make elsewhere (Cranton, 1992). These guidelines cover the planning, facilitating, and debriefing of a role play.

- The purpose or the learning goals of the role play should be clear to and agreed upon by all participants.
- The scenario should be as realistic as possible, preferably drawing on an experience familiar to the participants.

- Each player should have a clear description of the roles and the context within which the scenario takes place, but an actual script should not be used.
- Participation in the roles should be voluntary.
- Some individuals should act as observers, taking notes and preparing to discuss the activity from their point of view.
- The creative use of props and furniture can assist in establishing a realistic scenario.
- The length of the role play should be specified and fairly brief—five to ten minutes.
- It may be helpful for the educator to participate in the role play, especially if students are anxious about performing.
- Debriefing of a role play must be thoroughly and carefully done, beginning with the players reporting on their perspectives while they were in the roles.
- In the second part of the debriefing, observers can give their comments and perceptions, as well as ask questions of the role players.
- Finally in debriefing, the group as a whole has the opportunity to discuss the role play in relation to its purpose and goals.
- If communicative learning is to be facilitated, the group should come to a common understanding of what happened in the role play and what it meant to the players, the observers, and other members of the class.

Using Case Studies Effectively

Case studies can be used with any class size. Students can work on the cases individually or in small groups, in or out of the classroom. In some large business courses, case studies are the primary learning strategy. To facilitate communicative learning, however, follow collaborative rather than competitive procedures, and make it clear that the intent is not to produce one correct solution. The goal is to encourage discussion and shared inquiry, not to complete a task.

Some guidelines to consider in developing and using case studies are given here, based partly on Boyd's (1980) and Knox's (1986) suggestions.

- The learning goal for the case study needs to be clear and agreed upon by all participants.
- The case situation should be as realistic as possible and clearly relevant to the learning goal.
- The case situation can be one which has been experienced by some learners or the educator; it then can be developed in the group, or several cases can be designed by small groups and exchanged.
- Characters in the case should be portrayed in an interesting and genuine manner—they should have names, titles, and personalities.
- The necessary background information should be provided—for example, the relationships among people, the nature of the organization, or the social context.
- The case should be written in such a way that it does not suggest one solution is possible; in fact, it should be clear that several alternatives are feasible in the situation.
- Case studies usually contain leading questions for discussion at the end of the presentation; this may be as simple as asking, for example, "What should Sarah do now?" or it may involve a more complex set of questions that guide a group through the process of understanding the case.
- In debriefing case studies, individuals or small groups can present their perspectives on what could be done in the case situation and describe their reasoning.
- If possible (if the class is not too large), an attempt should be made to have the whole group come to a common understanding of the case situation.

Networks and Support Groups

Communicative learning is developed by working with others in discussions and group projects, and through the use of such strategies as role playing and case studies. Each of these approaches emphasizes the use of language to come to a common understanding of the nature of human beings in certain settings, communities, or cultures. The educator can further enhance communicative learning by encouraging students to develop networks and support groups outside the classroom, which perhaps may even continue after their course or program is finished. Such groups can develop spontaneously. For example, students who are involved in a meaningful discussion in class may continue the conversation in the cafeteria or call each other in the evening to clarify points made in class. We know we have succeeded in stimulating learners' interest and learning when this happens. However, we also can deliberately advocate these types of interactions in order to augment in-class activities.

Learner networks are sustained relationships among fellow learners. While these connections may be initiated in the classroom, they extend beyond it. For some students, they continue for months or even years after the course has ended. The primary purpose of networks is to exchange information, experiences, and ideas—the term, "network," also refers to groups of radio or television stations and to computer systems, ways of conveying information. Brookfield (1986) reports on research in which he surveyed successful independent learners and found that learner networks were the most important resource in their learning.

Similar to learner networks, support groups are sustained relationships among students, extending beyond the classroom. However, less emphasis is placed on exchange of information and more on personal and affective sharing and encouragement. Members of a support group share experiences in order to back and give strength to each other. They validate each other's thoughts and feelings and turn to each other when problems arise. There is a sense of caring for members of the group; friendships often form among individuals. Farquharson (1995) adds that support groups "strengthen the voice of learners and thus redress some of the inherent power imbalances that can exist in formal teaching relationships" (p. 95).

Encouraging Learner Networks

The formation of learner networks can be formally or informally encouraged during a course or program. The educator should not leave to chance alone a process which has such potential for facilitating communicative learning. Some of the following strategies are adapted from my suggestions for advocating learner networks in support of transformative learning (Cranton, 1994).

- Discuss the value of learner networks directly with the students throughout the course, recommending that such liaisons be set up.
- Provide students with ample opportunities to get to know each other well and work together over a period of time in small groups.
- Explicitly encourage project teams or groups who share the responsibility for completing a project outside of the classroom to develop learner networks.
- Encourage liaisons among learners by referring those who ask you questions to another learner who has experience and expertise in that area.
- Suggest an internet discussion group as the basis of a learner network or that students use e-mail to correspond with you and each other.
- Model your belief in the importance of networks by referring to those special interest groups or associations of which you are a member.

- Where relevant, encourage students to join professional associations, attend conferences, and participate in the larger community of scholars.

Promoting Support Groups

Support groups tend to emerge naturally when there is trouble. Students band together to face difficult examinations or to express their frustration about a poor learning experience. What we want to do, though, is promote support groups as a positive way to increase communicative understanding. When people support each other emotionally and personally, their communication deepens. Although we obviously cannot require people to care for each other, we can arrange class circumstances in such a way as to promote the development of positive support groups. Each of the suggestions given here may be relevant in different teaching contexts.

- Encouraging students to act as a unit in some cause or project can lead to the formation of cohesive and supportive groups. Even in a large class, learners can act as advocacy groups in a context appropriate to the course; for example, supporting an environmental issue, applying for project funding, or providing voluntary services in the community.

- When groups take responsibility for setting out and working toward their own learning goals, they may come to depend on each other for ideas, resources, and help.

- Eliminating competition for grades is appropriate in some contexts; self-evaluation conducted by learner groups furthers strong group development.

- If learners need to meet and do things together outside of the classroom, support groups can be cultivated—projects in the field such as reporting on a business operation or identifying plant life in a provincial park can form the basis of this.

- Forming groups based on psychological type or learning style can intensify the interpersonal relationships among members.

- In some courses, a retreat or weekend trip may be an appropriate way to strengthen relations among learners.

- Study groups, in which students meet outside of class time, can be a formal component of a course. If students choose their own group members, they may be more likely to form support groups from this beginning point. Setting up study groups based on compatible learning style or psychological type is not a good idea as each group would share the same strengths and weaknesses.

- Arranging social events with students can lead to group cohesiveness—a mid-term barbecue, a costume party for Halloween, or a meal together before or after class can do wonders in helping students get to know each other.

Summary

All our social systems have been constructed over time by people debating, questioning, and discussing values and issues with each other. In all organizations, communities, countries, and cultures, agreed-upon ways of behaving, moral codes, and taboos exist. What is proper in one culture may not be in another. What is an acceptable procedure in one organization may not be in another. Understanding this social world is communicative knowledge. Even though we tend to reify such knowledge and treat it as fixed, communicative knowledge is a product of shared inquiry and therefore open to flux and evolution.

By facilitating communicative learning among our students, we model the process of shared inquiry. Social behaviors and practices cannot be taught as though they are scientific facts. Educational strategies that emphasize dialogue and interaction must form the core of courses where communicative learning is the goal.

Through classroom discussion, students explore a diversity of perspectives, learn how to analyze and debate ideas, and benefit from each others' experiences. Planning meaningful discussion is more difficult than preparing an engaging lecture, because discussion cannot be predicted and controled. Nevertheless, advance planning and paying attention to the atmosphere of the class can go a long way to promoting good dialogue among students.

In collaborative group work, learners work together to create knowledge. They share experiences and ideas, pool resources, and thereby gain new insights. After initiating group work, the educator steps out of the hierarchical relationship with learners and becomes a part of the learning group. Care must be taken with the formation of the groups, the nature of the learning project, and the group process. Groups tend to go through regular developmental phases during which members establish their relationships with each other and set up group norms. The group develops its own operating communicative understanding.

Role plays and case studies are ways of simulating interactions that learners will experience in the world outside of the classroom. As such, both should be as realistic as possible, perhaps drawing on experiences of students or the teacher. Since role plays can be powerful and emotional, they require careful planning, facilitating, and debriefing. Case studies tend to be less dramatic, but allow for a greater breadth of understanding. Legal systems, educational systems, or organizational behavior can be comprehended through case studies.

Learner networks and support groups often emerge spontaneously during a course in response to demands placed on students or even as a reaction to negative experiences. Both are powerful learning strategies and should be actively and positively encouraged. In a network, information and resources are exchanged; in a support group, personal caring and empathy is the focus. Both types of connections extend beyond the duration of a course or program—it is one of the goals in higher education to produce continued learning and dialogue. By setting up circumstances that promote learner sharing of information, networks can be initiated. By providing opportunities for students to get to know each other as individuals both inside and outside the classroom, we can encourage the circumstances in which support groups might flourish.

Chapter Seven

Fostering Emancipatory Learning

Self-knowledge and freedom from constraint are fundamental human objectives. Education has always attempted to advance these goals through learning. Critical thinking, autonomy, self-directed learning, lifelong learning, and empowerment are among the ideals that institutions of higher education stand for. We all want our students to think for themselves, question what they read, take responsibility for their own learning, and learn how to learn. These goals are part of emancipatory learning.

As described in Chapter One, emancipatory learning takes place when students engage in critical self-reflection. This involves examining their existing knowledge, social systems, and personal lives with a critical eye. Such self-reflection can uncover distorted or incomplete knowledge, and emancipation results when individuals become aware of these errors or gaps and take freeing action. For example, I may believe that I have no skill in mathematics. But if I come to a point where I need to understand statistics, I must face my reluctance to work with figures. Through self-reflection I may recall a series of poor math teachers in my early years or perhaps a parent who told me that girls should not bother with math. This reveals my distorted assumptions. If I then go on to conquer statistics, and even enjoy mathematics, emancipation has taken place. I have freed myself from a constraint and become aware of a choice I can make. Prior to self-reflection, I had no choice, as I believed I could not learn mathematics; now I can choose whether or not to pursue the subject.

As teachers, we often tend to convey knowledge as we know it. We teach what we know to those students who have come to learn in our discipline. There is, as Kincheloe (1991, pp. 2021) describes it, a "cult of the expert." He sees this as "the myth that men and women should seek guidance from those blessed with society's credentials to direct them." By encouraging this, we maintain the status quo and standard practices in our field of study. Knowledge is produced by scholars far away from the teaching and learning setting and then transferred to those sitting in the classroom. Teaching is always a political activity; either we choose to maintain the systems within which we work or we encourage critical questioning of those systems (see for example, Brookfield, 1995; Kincheloe, 1991).

Encouraging critical questioning, and hence emancipatory learning, is one goal of higher education. Fine rhetoric, and easy enough to say, but how does a faculty member teaching introductory chemistry have time to worry about emancipatory learning when students are struggling daily with basic chemistry concepts? "I have too much material to cover," is the common response to such a suggestion. It is hard to add another responsibility onto an already over-burdened teaching load. But if we really want our students to become critical thinkers, responsible learners, and autonomous human beings, we must make efforts to those ends. If not, by only following the transfer-of-knowledge model, we may prevent potential learner empowerment.

In this chapter, I review a variety of strategies for fostering emancipatory learning, selecting methods appropriate for different disciplines and various levels of learning. Encouraging self-reflection through journals is described, and several alternative approaches to the use of journals are suggested. Critical debates and critical questioning are two valuable techniques. Tactics for encouraging students to articulate and examine their assumptions are included. Finally, since increasing autonomy and self-directed learning are at the heart of emancipatory learning, I include a separate section on these topics.

Critical Self-Reflection through Journal Writing

Journal writing has long been widely advocated as an effective way to increase reflective thinking. Historically, diaries provided a means of self-expression when other outlets were limited. We are all familiar with the journal-writing habits of people in the Victorian era. And we all know *The Diary of Anne Frank*, the writings of a young Jewish girl in hiding during World War II. In psychotherapy and analysis, journals are often recommended for increasing self-awareness (for example, see Progoff, 1983).

In education, journals are popular at every level and in almost every discipline, though the purpose is not always one of increasing critical self-reflection. In the health professions, students keep journals or logs related to their clinical experiences. In education, teachers-in-training write about their classroom practice. In English literature courses, learners record in journals their reactions and thoughts about readings. Journals are widely promoted in second language learning and in basic education or reentry programs. I even know of a faculty member who requires her large class of first-year chemistry students to keep a journal.

Journal writing allows students to record first what happened, then to step back from the experience and view it in a fresh way, and finally to question the value or importance of the experience. When it is approached in this fashion, journal writing is modeled on the content, process, and premise reflection questions described in Chapter One. What happened? How did it come to be this way? Why is this important in the first place? In her thesis, van Halen-Faber (1996) analyzed the logs of teacher trainees for, among other things, evidence of content, process, and premise reflection. Although she found less indication of premise reflection than the other two modes, she was able to identify each quite clearly.

Guidelines for Journal Writing

There are a variety of approaches to journal writing from which to choose. Selection depends on the nature of the course, class size, and the role that the journal is to play in the curriculum. Students should have as much say as possible in the style and format of their journal. The following are some options.

- Record what happened on one-half of the page and express thoughts, feelings, and questions on the other half.
- Write a journal in sections, e.g. a life history, a letter to a historical person, or dream analysis. (For an excellent example of dream interpretation in the context of learning, see MacKeracher, 1996.)
- Write on a different theme each week, based on experiences or discussions taking place in the classroom.
- Write from various perspectives; for example, pretend to be another person and write journal entries from that person's viewpoint.
- Keep a dialogue journal which is exchanged regularly with a partner or members of a small group for further comments, insights, and questions.
- Keep a dialogue journal to be submitted to the educator regularly for comments, insights, and questions.

- Keep a log of any unsolved problems or unresolved issues in the course; either exchange it with a partner or return to it regularly to work on the problems.
- After each class, write "What I learned," "What I did not learn," and "Why."
- Keep a multi-media journal, including photographs, clippings from papers, poetry, collages, and video or audiotape segments.

Students who are inexperienced with journal writing may find it hard to start at first or may be anxious about the process. Many questions about teacher expectations often arise, particularly if the instructor attempts to make the process flexible and give students plenty of choice. Even learners who have kept journals in previous courses may express hesitation or reluctance. We must discourage those students who try to find out what the teacher is looking for and reproduce that in a journal—this is not the path to critical reflection. We want students to take responsibility, make decisions about their learning, and engage in meaningful questioning. The following suggestions may be helpful in promoting journal writing that stimulates critical self-reflection.

- Helping students get started writing a journal can be critical. I am always surprised by the number of students who say, three or four weeks into a course, "I still intend to write a journal; I just haven't started yet." Walden (1995) suggest that list-making can be a useful starting-point technique for anxious or threatened learners. For example, students can list people who have influenced their lives or relevant experiences or things that need to be done. Most people are familiar with making lists, so anxiety is reduced. Later, the reasons for including items on the list can be questioned.
- A similar, though slightly more difficult, starting point is to suggest that students develop a list of key events or markers. Depending on the nature of the course, these might be life events, critical stages in becoming a

professional, or markers in the understanding of the
subject area (e.g., When did you get really confused?
When did you have an "ah-ha" moment?). Students
then go back and write about how and why each event
was a critical time.

- Encourage students to make journal entries at a regular time of the day or week. Otherwise, it is tempting
to treat the journal like many other assignments and
write it all at once when it is due. The time chosen
should be uninterrupted and consistent, allowing for
contemplation, review, emotional reaction, and the
wandering of the mind that leads one to critical self-reflection. For some students, this may involve curling
up on the sofa late at night and writing by hand in a
notebook, for others, an hour in front of the computer
on Saturday morning. It is important that the routine
is comfortable for the individual.

- Explaining the nature of content, process, and premise
reflection may be helpful for some learners. If students
think of what happened, how it came to be that way,
and why it is important, reflection is naturally fos-
tered. Some students may find it useful to discuss
these questions with a partner or a friend—we cannot
see the back of our heads by looking in a mirror (Brookfield, 1995), but if another person acts as a second mirror, we can see quite clearly.

- If dialogue journals are used and exchanged with
either a peer or the teacher, the person responding
needs to balance supportive and challenging comments. Writing such comments as "Good point" and "I
agree" in the margin of a journal is not enough. Positive comments should be specific and supplemented by
questions such as, "Why do you say this?" "Could you
describe when and how you developed this value?" "If
you took this line of thinking a little further, where
would it take you?"

- Generally, journals should not be graded. Grading
tends to lead to conformity, the antithesis of critical
self-reflection. If some form of evaluation is required,

learner self-evaluation is one alternative. Another is to base evaluation on the frequency of occurrences of premise reflection, regardless of all other attributes of the journal. The danger here is that students may be encouraged to invent examples of premise reflection to please the teacher. Writing style and grammar should never be included in the evaluation when the purpose of journal writing is to foster critical self-reflection.

• If students review, analyze, and interpret their journals at the end of a course or at mid-term and again at end-of-term, critical reflection is further nurtured. Looking back over previous thoughts and reactions can provide a fresh perspective, especially when considerable learning and change has taken place. Questioning our thoughts of last month can be easier than questioning how we think today.

Critical Debate and Critical Questioning

Emancipatory learning is a process of identifying taken-for-granted assumptions, examining them, and gaining a fresh perspective. This is not an easy thing to do. It is more comfortable to leave assumptions, values, and beliefs unquestioned. Thus, the educator who fosters emancipatory learning may run into the natural human tendency to resist change. In addition we want our students to enjoy our courses; we do not want them to be hurt, angry, or frustrated. We know that we should not force people into disturbing situations for their own good. Yet, we also believe we should encourage learners to challenge their beliefs, become aware of options and alternatives, and see things in a different way. This is an awkward dance.

Critical debate and critical questioning are two strategies that encourage reflection; they neither place the educator in an aggressive position, nor the students in an overwhelming situation. In critical debates (Brookfield, 1990), students argue for a position that is contrary to one they hold personally. It is a form of role reversal to present a position counter to one's own convictions. Because it is set up as a structured debate, the process resembles a game and is therefore less threatening, although it is still a difficult exercise for students to undertake. In critical questioning (Brookfield, 1987; Cranton, 1994), students are encouraged to become their own questioners and develop habits of critical reflection independent of the educator. Content (What), process (How), and premise (Why) reflection questions can form the basis of this process. Effective critical questioning requires sensitivity and insight on the part of the teacher, but it is well worth the effort and time.

Structuring Provocative Critical Debates

The critical debate requires that learners take a position with which they disagree. Brookfield (1990, pp. 129-130) provides instructions for setting up such a debate.

- Devise a motion on a controversial issue that inspires strong feelings and divergent opinions among students.

- Ask students to volunteer to speak for or against this motion. Students will select the side that most closely matches their own viewpoint.

- Now ask students to reverse their chosen preference. All those who volunteered to speak for the motion should speak against it and vice versa.

- Explain clearly why such a course of action is being taken. Stress the benefits of arguing against the view one already holds. Point out that the best way of defending one's ideas is to have a full understanding and appreciation of the opposing view.

- Give clear instructions about the time of the exercise. Brookfield suggests 90 minutes for a full debate and debriefing, but this may be reduced.

- Form two teams, one to support the motion and one to oppose it. Give the teams time to prepare their arguments.
- Give each team a specified time (5 to 10 minutes) to present their arguments.
- Give the teams a few minutes to prepare rebuttals.
- Give each team a specified time (about 5 minutes) to present their rebuttals.
- After the debate and with the whole group encourage participants to discuss the experience of arguing for beliefs and ideas that they do not personally hold.

This last exercise, which constitutes the debriefing of the debate, requires care and understanding. Some students may have been frustrated by the activity or have had other unpleasant emotional reactions. Surprisingly, some students change their minds on an issue about which they felt strongly at the beginning of the debate. When this happens, give learners ample opportunity to talk about the process as it can be quite disconcerting to find oneself doing a turnabout on an issue.

In addition to using a structured critical debate, educators can encourage learners to engage in short impromptu role reversals in the midst of a discussion. Suggesting that two students arguing different sides of an issue reverse sides for a minute or two can spark interest in exploring an alternative perspective. If this strategy is used frequently during discussion, students become quite competent at taking a position counter to the one they hold. This is exactly what we hope for in fostering emancipatory learning.

Promoting Skillful Critical Questions

We often ask questions of students during a lecture or discussion in order to encourage their involvement or capture their attention, without giving much thought to the nature of the questions. Questions designed to elicit information or opinions are fairly easy to formulate. When the purpose is to encourage critical reflection, we need to pay more attention to what kinds of questions we ask, work on designing and asking good questions, and, most importantly, promote students' critical questioning of themselves and each other. Brookfield (1987) notes that one needs training, as well as a substantial amount of experience, to be a good critical questioner. However, as long as the less-experienced educator does not venture too far into personal issues or take an aggressive approach, critical questioning can be learned on the job.

Some of the guidelines given here are adapted from Brookfield (1987, pp. 93-97). Not all suggestions are relevant for all teaching contexts, but, generally, critical questioning is a strategy that can be applied in any subject area and at any level.

Brookfield suggests focusing questions on specific events, situations, people, and actions. Asking such general, open-ended questions as "What is your philosophy of nursing practice?" is threatening and intimidating, as well as very difficult to answer. On the other hand, asking students to describe, for example, a situation in which they were satisfied with their performance is likely to yield responses that can be further pursued. If one nursing student responds that she was pleased when a patient praised her, the educator can ask what it means when a patient praises a nurse. Is patient contentment an important indicator of good nursing? If another student responds that she is most satisfied when a patient questions her or refuses medication without knowing all of the side effects, the educator can pursue this. Is it important that patients think for themselves or is it best if they comply with the nurse's orders?

In a similar fashion, teachers can start with the basic "What happened?" question. This can be asked in relation to a field experience, a videotape, or a reading: Tell me what you experienced or saw or read. This initiates content reflection, which is focused on a specific event. After students answer with a description, the next level of questioning is: How did it come to be this way? How did the author of the reading come to that conclusion? How did the videotape convey the story? How did people in the field come to do it that way? Here, process reflection is evoked by the same event. Questioning can then be extended to the premise of the experience—why is this important anyway? Why do we care about this topic? What if this article had never been written, would it make any difference to our lives? Why do we use antibiotics in the first place? How would we be better off if we did not use them? Asking students to imagine the world without something is a good strategy for encouraging premise reflection. Why do we have schools? How would the world be without them? Why do we have a police force? What would a society without one be like? Why do we care about exploring space? What difference would it make if we never had?

Brookfield (1987) also suggests working from the particular to the general in critical questioning. He therefore recommends not initially asking abstract or conceptual questions. He believes people are more comfortable with questions that focus on the details of individual incidents. However, when psychological type preferences are taken into account, it is clear that this is not the case for all learners. Some individuals prefer more global or theoretical discussions and are frustrated by focusing solely on details. Use a variety of types of questions, keeping different learning styles in mind.

Critical questioning needs to take place within an atmosphere that is supportive and comfortable. The tone should be conversational and the questions relatively free of jargon, except in situations where all students know the specialized language of the discipline and already use it freely. The questioning process should not resemble an interview or, worse, an interrogation. In the classroom, students should be encouraged to question each other as frequently as the teacher questions the students. The more the critical questioning process takes the form of a discussion or conversation, the more likely it is that learners will express and examine their beliefs and assumptions regarding the topic. The eventual goal is for students to develop the ability and desire to question themselves apart from and independent of the educator and other students.

Articulating and Examining Assumptions

Each of the strategies presented in this chapter has as an aim the articulation and examination of assumptions. Journals, critical debates, and critical questioning are methods suited to almost any discipline in higher education. Other methods can be equally effective, but may be more limited in their application. Here, I suggest some alternative techniques, indicating where each could be used.

Critical Incidents

The critical incident strategy was originally developed as a research technique in the social sciences (Flanagan, 1954). Since then, it has become a widely used educational activity, especially in the promotion of critical thinking (Brookfield, 1995; Cranton, 1992, 1994). Students are asked to describe, in writing, a significant experience or event, either positive or negative. The descriptions usually include who was involved in the incident, when and where it happened, what made it unusually positive or negative, and what insights were gained from the experience. Students then analyze the incident, looking for assumptions or implicit expressions of values. This is best done in pairs or small groups, as the discussion and questioning of peers helps learners discover in the incident what they may not be able to see on their own. Only if the event is highly personal or if learners are reluctant to share them should the analysis be done independently.

The following example was used during a course in a social work program:

> *Directions:* Think back over the last two months of your work placement. Was there a time when you thought you could not go on any longer? A time when you decided you were in the wrong profession? A time when you wished you were anywhere else but there? Describe that incident briefly. Who was involved? Where did it happen? Why was it such a difficult experience? What would you do differently in a similar situation in the future?

A student response might state: "My placement was in a senior's home. I had this one lovely lady that I had been visiting a lot. She liked it when I read to her. I would look for interesting articles and stories and bring them in for my visit. One day I took a poem. I thought it would be neat if she read it to some of the other ladies—it was a poem about being old, it was beautiful, and I thought it wouldn't sound right if I read it. I called some of the other ladies over and handed my client the poem and asked her to read it. She looked at it for awhile and then handed it back to me and silently wheeled herself out of the room. It took me a few minutes to realize she couldn't read. I never felt so bad as I did then."

An analysis of this incident might have revealed the following assumptions: everyone can read, anyone wants to read aloud to others, being old is beautiful, and a young person cannot share the words of an old person. Discussion of the incident among a small group might uncover more related assumptions, as well as those of other members of the group.

Simulations and Games

Simulations are hypothetical, but usually realistic situations created and worked through in the classroom. They need to be carefully designed if they are to reveal students' assumptions, beliefs, and values. Games are usually more abstract and are not intended to simulate a real experience directly. Some dimensions of a game are often drawn from reality—chess as a battle, for example. Games also differ from simulations in that they have winners and losers. Although they are more difficult to use as a means of stimulating critical reflection, when one finds the right game for the right context, it can be an exciting and motivating strategy. Computer games are becoming an intriguing resource for faculty.

I recently observed an effective simulation in a college class on community development. Students knew in advance that there was to be a simulation that day, but had been given nothing special to prepare. Talking in role the instructor said, "I am the consultant whom you invited to meet with you today. Jane wrote to me, who is Jane, here?" Jane identified herself. The instructor went on to describe the simulation without ever leaving her role as consultant. The class became a group of concerned citizens who wanted to develop a Meals-on-Wheels program in their community. The instructor soon had the class divided into committees, each responsible for a part of the planning of the program. She brought out resources on nutrition, financial statements, a large map of the town, and plenty of paper for the planning committees. Students assumed roles as the need arose—"I have a trucking company," one student shouted out, when transportation was required.

In the ensuing discussion, a multitude of assumptions, related to community power structures, empowerment of citizens, economic issues, and social class, were articulated and questioned. It takes courage to use a simulation in this fashion, and many instructors would probably prefer to provide more structure in advance, as well as assign roles to individual students. The same simulation could have been conducted with a detailed handout.

Poetry, Metaphors, and Collages

For some students and in some contexts, drawing on their intuitive side is an excellent way to bring out values, beliefs, and assumptions. Not everyone responds to the analytical approach that underlies transformative learning theory. Boyd and Myers (1988), writing from a Jungian perspective, use the term *discernment*, rather than critical reflection, to describe the process of becoming aware of one's assumptions. Discernment is seen to be an inner journey and a dialogue with the unconscious. Whether or not we agree with this particular interpretation of the process, we probably can agree that it is not always a rational one.

Both reading and writing poetry can be ways of externalizing deep feelings and values. Students are asked to select a poem that portrays their reactions to a specific issue, then read this poem to the class or to a smaller group (if necessary, provide collections to select from). Their choice can be interpreted in relation to the values expressed, the images conveyed, or the overall mood of the poem. Students can gain powerful insights from the discussion of why they chose a certain poem to read. For example, a student might select Margaret Atwood's *Elegy for the Giant Tortoises* in response to an environmental issue, and read the lines:

> on the road where I stand they will materialize,
> plodding past me in a straggling line

awkward without water
their small heads pondering
from side to side, their useless armor
sadder than tanks and history

(Atwood, 1976, p. 56).

In discussion, learners could explore the use of images of armor and war in relation to endangered species or the vision of tortoises materializing on a road. The main question to be posed is what aspects of the poem reflect assumptions that the student holds. This activity could call on other art forms as well—paintings, music, photography, or sculptures.

Writing poetry is more intimidating than selecting and reading poetry, but can be a freeing and inspirational activity. In a poem we can express our unconscious or untamed imagination—we can say things that we would not dare to say in conventional prose. A poem often expresses things in unusual ways with no constraints of format or structure. Instead of selecting a poem to read, students write a poem (it need only be a few lines) related to an issue in the course. In small groups or pairs, the poem can be interpreted in terms of the underlying assumptions it reveals.

Metaphors may be easier for students to work with than poetry and can unleash the same creative energy. Deshler (1990) describes a detailed process of metaphor analysis which I have adapted and simplified for use as a class activity. The instructor begins with one or two warm-up metaphors to encourage students to start thinking in this fashion. For example, "Life is..." or "Marriage is..." may be put up on a flip chart or whiteboard. The class then engages in brainstorming to produce as many varied metaphors as possible. In brainstorming, no judgments are made and each contribution is recorded. One response tends to stimulate other responses in a similar vein. If the metaphors are slow to come initially, the instructor should be prepared to give several examples—Marriage is... a prison, a haven, a puzzle, a circus, a picnic, a pizza. When metaphors for the example are exhausted, the instructor introduces the concept relevant to the course content for which metaphors will be produced: for example, Qualitative research is...; Mathematics is...; Learning is.... The concept chosen should be one for which it is important to discover learners' underlying assumptions. Do they assume qualitative research to be less valid than quantitative research? Do they assume mathematics to be very abstract and theoretical?

The metaphors are then analyzed. The educator asks, "What are the characteristics of a circus that are similar to the characteristics of a marriage?" Learners might list such ideas as: confusing, exciting, colorful, chaotic, unpredictable, dangerous, abusive, good for children, exotic. With a group this list is often quite long and contains a mixture of individual student's values.

In the final part of the activity, students work in small groups or pairs to determine the underlying assumptions or values revealed by their metaphors. It is best here if students work with their own metaphor and help each other to unpack and question it. The individual who suggested "picnic" as a metaphor for marriage might be assuming that it is fun but short-lived or that it is a continuous, happy time. Only the person who selected the metaphor can confirm whether the assumption is true of the way he or she feels. Metaphors have a way of revealing values and attitudes of which a person is not normally conscious. We use metaphors in speech continually and increasing our awareness of their use is an intriguing means of fostering critical self-reflection.

Elementary school teachers are familiar with the use of collages, but how often do we see them being created in higher education classrooms? I was introduced to the use of collages by two early childhood teachers who were enroled in one of my adult education classes, and I have incorporated this strategy into several courses since that time. If creating a collage is to lead to the articulation of assumptions and values, a theme should be chosen with this goal in mind. For example, learners might be asked to represent how they see their profession in a collage or what they have learned throughout their course. Collages are effective as closing activities in a course or program. Students may work on them individually or in small groups, depending on the purpose of the exercise.

The students and instructor bring to class old magazines, scissors, glue sticks, colored paper, and colored pens. With the theme in mind, students create a collage of any size or shape (some may even be three-dimensional). If, at first, some individuals feel foolish or threatened by the creative nature of the task, be supportive but otherwise leave them on their own. These reactions usually vanish when everyone becomes involved. The educator should participate in the activity, creating her or his own collage, or working with a group if the exercise is being done in groups.

A collage activity may be examined in a number of ways. The finished results can be posted on walls for everyone to look at. Students can discuss their collage with a partner, explaining what they intended to convey by the words and images included. Each collage can be presented to the class by its creator as other students ask questions and give their insights into its meaning. Surprisingly, learners nearly always discover things in their collage that they had not initially set out to express. In this way the activity has value by helping people express their beliefs to others.

Increasing Self-Direction and Autonomy

When learners reflect on their assumptions and beliefs through any of the strategies presented here, and when that reflection leads to the realization that their assumptions may be limiting or that alternative perspectives exist, they free themselves from the constraint of incomplete knowledge. We cannot predict what will spark such reflection for any student: it can be a comment made in a journal, a question asked by the teacher or a fellow student, or an insight gained during a class activity. Our goal as educators is to provide as many opportunities as possible for critical self-reflection to be stimulated.

One product of critical self-reflection is increased learner self-direction and autonomy. This is not a one-way street by any means—growth in self-direction and autonomy likewise enhances critical self-reflection. It is important for the educator who is interested in fostering emancipatory learning to be aware of this.

Self-Directed Learning

Self-directed learning is conceived of in several different ways in the literature. Knowles (1975) first popularized the term more than twenty years ago. His concept of self-directed learning involves students making decisions about the design and implementation of their learning. They decide what they need to learn, set objectives, choose methods, find resources, and evaluate their own progress. The help of others, including teachers, may or may not be a part of the process. This definition remains popular today and is usually what practitioners mean when they refer to self-directed courses or programs.

In the late 1970s and 1980s, some writers and researchers began to describe self-directedness as a characteristic of people. This led to attempts to measure how self-directed students are or how ready they are to engage in self-directed learning (Guglielmino, 1977; Oddi, 1984). Although these and other similar instruments have been widely used, they have also been heavily criticized. It is questionable whether self-directedness can be quantified, considered as a one-dimensional variable, or freed from the learning and social context. In her doctoral thesis, Pilling-Cormick (1996) attempts to address some of these complex questions, but in general, this area remains murky.

Brookfield (1986) challenges the ways in which Knowles' work has been interpreted by practitioners, arguing that not all students are capable of self-directed learning and that educators should not put themselves in the position of responding only to learners' expressed needs. Candy (1991) synthesizes and integrates the work on self-directed learning into a large and comprehensive text. He concludes that there are four facets to the concept: personal autonomy (having freedom of choice), learner control (organizing one's own learning in a formal setting), self-management (conducting one's own education), and autodidaxy (engaging in independent learning projects).

Each facet in Candy's model is related to our work as educators in fostering emancipatory learning. When students are able to reflect critically on the knowledge they acquire, their social context, or their personal lives, they gain personal autonomy. Critical reflection leads to freedom of choice; similarly, freedom of choice enhances critical reflection. Students who have acquired the habit of questioning are also more likely to be able to take control over decisions about their learning within a formal course or program and to manage their own educational paths. One would likewise expect the reflective learner to more readily pursue autodidactic or independent learning projects outside of the classroom. Personal autonomy, learner control, self-management, and autodidactic learning are all goals of higher education. They are both conditions and consequences of emancipatory learning.

Autonomy

Although personal autonomy is viewed as one facet of self-directed learning, it is a broader concept than this, and, as such, deserves further attention here. Freedom to act and free will have long been of interest to philosophers, as well as educators. Historically, autonomy has been a central tenet of higher education, although this is now changing as universities and colleges respond to social and economic developments. Still, as teachers in higher education, we expect and work toward having freedom to act and free will ourselves; we hope that our students also work toward this ideal.

Drawing on the writing of philosophers, Candy (1991, pp. 108-109) describes an individual as having autonomy to the extent that he or she:

- conceives of goals and plans independently;
- exercises freedom of choice in thought and action;
- makes judgments on the basis of morally defensible beliefs;
- has the will and capacity to carry through plans of action;
- exercises self-mastery in the face of setbacks; and,
- has a concept of himself or herself as autonomous.

Jarvis (1992) discusses the concepts of free will and freedom to act, pointing out the paradoxes inherent in our understanding of freedom. When we have free will, we could have made a decision to act other than the one that was reached—we have options and we know we have options. However, many decisions are not made consciously; we do not think that much about what we decide to do. Even more limiting, many of our decisions are made because we have been programmed to think in a certain

way by our prior learning. People are not free from previous experience, including socialization. Jarvis presents
this as a paradox. When we learn, we restrict future
choices as that learning programs us in a certain way. On
the other hand, free will makes it possible for new learning to occur. If this were not the case, we would only learn
things that validate our current perspectives. It is important that students realize that they have free will and
equally critical that educators challenge students to go
beyond the constraints of prior learning.

We may have free will, but curtailed freedom to act.
Jarvis (1992) uses concepts of public and private space to
explain the restrictions on our freedom to act. In public
space, individuals must conform to the laws and regula-
tions of the state and society, or be punished in some way.
In private space, one has the freedom to act as one pleases.
However, changes in our society have led to a shrinking
of private space and much of what we do is done in a space
controled or owned by others. Even in private space,
people are not free of the influence of those in control, nor
are they free of social pressures to conform. In our classrooms, the space is generally controled by the teachers
who have power over that domain by virtue of their
position. We can hear this in the language we use—"my
classroom," "my students," and "my course." We see ourselves as owning the space in which education takes place,
thereby curtailing students' freedom to act.

Jarvis argues that when students have the desire to
exercise free will and when the control of the space is
delegated by the teacher to the students, limited autonomy exists. When learners have both control over the
space in which they learn and the desire to exercise free
will, they have autonomy. The message for educators is
that if we want to foster emancipatory learning, we need
at the very least to delegate control over the learning
experience to students. Jarvis (1992, p. 133) suggests that

when this is the case, "self-directed learning is a teaching technique rather than a learning strategy," implying that true self-directed learning takes place only outside of the classroom setting. This would mean that Candy's (1991) autodidactic learning would be the only one in which learners were autonomous, a debatable point. However, in some circumstances, educators can work toward actually giving up control of the space, instead of delegating it, by becoming a part of the group and a co-learner.

Summary

In higher education, we try to free students from the constraint of lack of knowledge, from lack of awareness of alternative ways of viewing the world. Whether we work in the sciences, social sciences, humanities, professions, or trades and technologies, we are always concerned with students' abilities to be critical, to question, and to be actively involved in seeking choices. This is what we mean when we say we are fostering emancipatory learning.

No one set of teaching strategies can produce the critical self-reflection that leads to emancipatory learning. Even when close questioning and careful thought are emphasized and conventional wisdom is challenged, it is ultimately the student's responsibility to engage in that kind of learning. All we can do is provide the opportunities, create the challenges, and support the process. Some effective methods can be used in virtually any discipline. Writing journals is a strategy that has considerable potential for fostering critical reflection, especially when it is combined with questioning, dialogue, or writing from a variety of perspectives. Critical debates, in which students argue for a position opposed to one they hold, can be a provocative catalyst for reflection. Similarly, asking critical questions of students and encouraging them to question each other can raise their consciousness regarding almost any issue—What happened? How did it come to be that way? Why is it important in the first place?

Critical incidents, simulations and games, poetry, metaphors, and collages can be used in some contexts and subjects. Each technique is designed to help learners articulate and question their assumptions and beliefs. Using poetry, metaphor, and collage draws on intuition or creativity, instead of reason and analysis, and therefore provides a fresh approach to critical reflection.

Emancipatory learning leads to increased learner self-direction and autonomy. At the same time, self-directed learning and the opportunity to be autonomous foster emancipatory learning. Educators need to support learners in the exercise of free will and give up control in order to allow them the freedom to act. Gaining autonomy is at the heart of higher education.

Chapter Eight

Evaluating Learning and Teaching

In higher education, we are answerable to our students, the employers of our students, the community, the public who funds us, and our own institutions. Thus, we are responsible for monitoring and communicating how well we are meeting our teaching and learning goals to all these constituents. As demand grows for greater accountability in our colleges and universities, the importance of evaluation increases. It is through the process of evaluation that we discover how well or poorly we are doing.

In some countries, quality assurance models, adapted from business and industry, are applied to teaching and learning in an effort to document the quality of faculty work (Eggins, 1997). Other countries impose strict examination procedures for the assessment of student learning to prove that universities are doing their job (Ume and Nworgu, 1997). Although we may oppose such strategies and fear their adoption or spread, evaluation in North America is still primarily the responsibility of individual faculty members. As such, it is crucial that we conduct thoughtful, valid, and meaningful evaluations of student learning and our own teaching. If we do not do it well, we may have the job taken away from us. As faculty autonomy is already eroding, this further loss would be unfortunate.

In Chapter Four, I describe three general evaluation strategies and loosely link their use with the kinds of learning we hope to foster in students. Objectively scored assessments are used to judge the acquisition of instrumental knowledge. Subjectively rated evaluations are appropriate for judging the quality of understanding a student has reached. Learner self-evaluations are most relevant for emancipatory learning with its goals of furthering individual empowerment and social change. Since knowledge of teaching is both communicative and emancipatory, subjectively rated methods and teacher self-reports are called for in the evaluation of instruction.

It is important to dispute the widely held idea that only objective evaluation is valid and reliable. This arises from the belief that the methods and measurements of science can and should be imposed on all forms of knowledge and understanding. The attempt to objectify or quantify social and personal knowledge does not make it more valid, and, in fact, tends to destroy its meaning altogether. I recently received a query from a Faculty of Health Sciences where innovative approaches, such as self-directed learning and small group methods, are in place; they were concerned about the subjective nature of the evaluation of such learning. It is to refute this kind of thinking that I present the arguments of this chapter.

I first approach the evaluation of learning in two ways: providing feedback to students and giving meaningful evaluations. By providing feedback, I mean giving the kind of evaluative information that does not count toward grades, but rather has as its sole purpose enhancement of learning. While this is sometimes called formative evaluation, the distinction between formative and summative evaluation has become blurred. In most courses, the so-called formative evaluations are tallied up to produce a final grade or summative evaluation. In the section on giving meaningful evaluations, I discuss strategies for assessing learning that do contribute to a grade or report.

I devote a separate section of the chapter to learner self-evaluation as this is a relatively new and controversial technique in higher education. Finally, I turn to the evaluation of teaching through the use of teaching dossiers. In each part of the chapter, I maintain the distinction between instrumental, communicative, and emancipatory learning, and indicate different evaluation strategies for each.

Providing Feedback to Students

We all require feedback in order to learn. In some independent learning projects, we obtain feedback as a result of our actions. For example, in learning to use a new computer software package, we immediately see the outcome of our attempts and can amend our response accordingly. In classroom learning, students often rely on comments and reactions from the instructor for feedback. Effective teacher response is a powerful learning stimulus for students. However, careless or insensitive feedback can destroy students' belief in their own abilities or even cause them to change their choice of studies. We probably all remember the impact of the teacher's red pen from our student days! Given how difficult it is to provide effective feedback, it is not surprising that educators consider evaluation to be the most problematic and difficult aspect of their work.

Brookfield (1990) suggests several characteristics of good feedback, most of which are relevant to learning in any domain.

- Feedback should be clear, referring to specific actions, behaviors, or ideas of the students and should be expressed in ordinary language.
- Feedback should be given as quickly as possible. When students are performing a task, feedback should be immediate. Comments on journals or other written material should be given back to students from one class to another, if possible.

- Feedback should be regular. Sometimes it is tempting to ignore the students who are doing well and focus on those who obviously need help, but everyone benefits from feedback.
- Teachers should be accessible for further discussion after feedback.
- Feedback needs to be individualized; comments should refer to the student personally. Response should not be such that learners suspect teachers of drawing from a list of pre-packaged comments. The standard, "good point," written in the margin quickly loses all meaning.
- Feedback should always contain some positive comments.
- Feedback should include suggestions for further study.
- Teachers should be able to justify their feedback. Whether affirming or critical, feedback must never be based on an educator's personal likes and dislikes.
- The goal of feedback is always to further learning. As well as providing positive or negative response to student work, it must give guidance for continued learning.

In addition to these general suggestions, feedback should be tailored to the specific type of learning involved. When the purpose of instruction is to convey instrumental knowledge and technical skills, feedback should indicate whether or not the response is correct. In this domain, theories, principles, facts, and procedures are clearly right or wrong. If a student performs a task and makes a mistake based on incorrect or missing information, this should be cleared up as quickly as possible.

When the goal is to facilitate communicative learning, feedback takes a different form. In this domain, knowledge is constructed during discourse and validated through consensus. The optimal conditions for participation in discourse, listed in Chapter Six, provide us with some guidance. Through feedback, the teacher can attempt to see that students have complete information, are free from self-deception, weigh evidence carefully, are open to alternatives, question presuppositions, have an equal opportunity to participate, and accept consensus as an indicator of validity. Here, feedback often takes the form of questioning during discussion in order to stimulate further thought: "Have you thought about it from this angle?" "Did you read this related article on the topic?" "How would you support the statement you are making here?" Praise that identifies insightful interpretation, and criticism that pinpoints faulty arguments also help learners progress toward a communicative learning goal.

Providing appropriate feedback to foster emancipatory learning may be the trickiest job of all. We need to be especially careful not to impose our own values or preferred choices on students. Brookfield (1990) and others argue that evaluation is necessarily value-laden and that education is always directive, which cannot be denied. But the purpose of emancipatory learning is to uncover alternatives and choices; therefore, it is illogical to judge the direction a student chooses. Feedback must lead students to question their own assumptions and engage in critical self-reflection. As such, it must maintain a balance between supportive comments and challenging questions. Students should not be judged, but rather encouraged to consider the source of their values and assumptions, as well as the consequences of maintaining their views. For example, in a sociology course, one could ask why we generally consider it reasonable to kill a complete stranger in war, but not an abusive spouse. Or, in an environmental issues course, the educator could ask students to question why in our country we eat cows, but not horses, and to relate that value to our land use. Feedback is not judgmental, but instead encourages students to review why they hold certain beliefs. When students do engage in critical reflection on various issues, the educator praises and pushes the process a little further.

The emancipatory learning process often produces strong emotional reactions. It is difficult and often painful to reflect on values or beliefs that have long been unquestioned. When deeply held, personal values are examined in such courses as life skills, communications, or women's studies, students may require much more supportive feedback than in courses where the critical questioning centers on epistemic perspectives. Educators need to be sensitive to students who are struggling emotionally and provide support themselves or arrange for it via learner networks. Challenging feedback should not be offered when a student is vulnerable. We have all seen those films in which a tough, demanding professor pushes on despite a student's tears and dramatically alters her life, but this is dangerous indeed for those of us not equipped with counseling skills.

Giving Meaningful Evaluations

When student learning must be evaluated for reporting and grading purposes, it is difficult not to rely on objective measures. This is especially hard to do when everyone around us—students, administrators, registrars, professional associations, graduate admissions committees—insists on objective evaluations. In general, objective and empirical methods are still valued and respected more than subjective and interpretive methods. Here, I ask that these views be questioned.

Objective means "existing in fact or in physical reality; independent of the observer, particularly independent of observer bias; *outside the body* [emphasis added]; in the environment; pertaining to an object" (Chaplin, 1985, p. 309). On the other hand, subjective means "pertaining to or dependent on a subject; dependent upon individual interpretation or accessible only to private experience" (Chaplin, 1985, p. 453). No doubt, many of our learning goals in higher education are objective in nature, but some are not. If I learn to repair lawn mowers through a course in small engine repair, this knowledge is publicly observable and objective in nature. If I gain self-confidence in working with engines or accept that my fear of machinery was a product of my upbringing, this is subjective knowledge. It was gained, at least in part, through the acquisition of objective knowledge, but my feeling of self-confidence is interpreted to be such by myself.

In a discussion of Habermas's thoughts, Held (1980) comments on the way in which we attempt to impose technical assessment onto values. We see this in, for example, the delegation of decision making to computers and the applications of automatic analysis and action systems to complex human environments. In other words, we first separate objective from subjective and then view objective as superior. We then use objectivity to eliminate subjectivity. This is precisely what we are trying to do when we argue that all evaluation should be objective.

Objectively Scored Evaluation

When instrumental knowledge or technical skills are evaluated, objectively scored assessment procedures are appropriate. Multiple-choice tests, true-false items, short answer tests, and checklists are familiar formats. The following guidelines for developing and using objectively scored evaluation procedures may be helpful (adapted from Cranton, 1989).

- Design questions to measure specific learning goals.
- Indicate in advance to students what goals will be assessed and which testing formats will be used.
- Describe in advance how much each test contributes toward a final grade.
- Present one clearly stated problem or question per item.

- Use simple language; avoid vague or convoluted wording.
- Be sure that each question has only one right answer.
- In a checklist, design each item so that it is answerable in a yes/no format.
- Avoid jargon unless students are expected to know the terms.
- Avoid complex grammatical structures, including double negatives.
- Organize items in a logical sequence.
- Present questions in a visually attractive manner.
- Indicate the scoring points or weight of questions.
- Provide clear directions in writing and repeat them orally.
- Ensure that adequate time is provided.
- Ensure that the facilities and resources are suitable.

Basically, objectively scored assessments should be kept as clear, simple, and straightforward as possible, regardless of the format. Long and complicated multiple-choice items with combinations of responses, such as "a and b, but not c, are correct" and "a, c, and d, but not b, are correct," or trick true-and-false items do not ensure accurate assessment. Even though such items appear frequently, including on professional certification examinations, they are not valid measurement techniques. In fact, it is more likely that they really evaluate students' test-taking experience rather than their learning.

Subjectively Rated Evaluation

The evaluation of students' communicative learning—their understanding of themselves, others, and the social world—must be subjective. Subjective evaluation includes the familiar written essay, term paper, or report. Case studies and problem-solving exercises are used in some disciplines. A performance or product created by students may also be evaluated. In some cases, students' oral presentations or discussions can be rated. Journals and log books can be subjectively evaluated, but not if they are used for emancipatory learning goals, as was discussed in Chapter Seven.

Good subjective evaluation and the ratings so engendered are trustworthy and credible (for example, see Patton, 1990). In accepting this form of evaluation, we rely on the expertise, professionalism, and credibility of the educators or other raters involved. Also, we rely on negotiation, agreement, and consensus among individuals—perhaps different raters, or teacher and student. The criticism that bias is inevitable, which is frequently applied to subjective ratings, is irrelevant here. We do have inclinations, beliefs, or tendencies (biases) that become a part of the evaluation process. Evaluations are based on our interpretations, rather than detached from them. The experience, knowledge, and professionalism of the evaluator inform the interpretations.

The following guidelines for developing and using subjectively rated evaluation procedures may be useful.

- There should be agreement between educator (or educators, if evaluation is being conducted for a program) and students that the nature of the learning goal is communicative.

- There should be agreement among all concerned as to what is being evaluated, and this should be described clearly.

- Those individuals providing ratings—educators and perhaps other professionals in the field—must be subject experts with established and respected credentials.

- Evaluators must be ethical, caring, responsible, and determined to evaluate fairly.

- Educators and students should accept that many factors and perspectives are involved in the evaluation process, and no final and absolute truth is possible.

- Whenever feasible, more than one person should evaluate the same student output.

- Whenever feasible, the same student learning should be evaluated by more than one method (e.g., observation of student performance in the field and a written report by the student).

- Maintaining a holistic perspective is helpful (i.e., keeping in mind the situation, background, and characteristics of the students).

- Educators should carefully identify the specific aspects, components, or characteristics to be evaluated (e.g., writing style, creativity, professionalism, caring attitude) and how each is demonstrated; these should be discussed with students.

- Developing a checklist, matrix, or framework for comments or ratings helps ensure that all important aspects are included in the evaluation.

- Referring to a good essay or an excellent performance during evaluation is sometimes useful.

- If one piece of evaluative evidence does not agree with most of the data, it should not be ignored, and the evaluation results should be questioned.

- The evaluation process, including its underlying philosophy and methods used, should be clearly understood and agreed upon by the students.

- Discussion and negotiation should occur between teacher and students regarding evaluation results—ideally, there should be consensus.

Subjectively rated evaluations rely heavily on the expertise and skill of the teacher, but then, so do objectively scored evaluations. A poorly constructed multiple-choice test that does not adequately represent the goals of the course is just as unfair as a hasty rating of an essay. Perhaps it is even more unfair, as the use of an objective test gives the illusion of precision. In general, when evaluating subjectively, we need to be careful, clear about what we are doing, open to a variety of perspectives and explanations, and engage in discussion and negotiation with others.

Many colleges and universities require numerical grades, which can be difficult to derive from a subjective evaluation. How do we decide that a student has demonstrated that she knows 85% of what she should know? When the knowledge itself cannot be quantified, teachers face a quandary. We need to think of numerical grades as ratings, rather than as a representation of the proportion of objectives mastered, as is done in the instrumental domain. The use of a rating scale, checklist, matrix, or some other framework facilitates the rating process.

Assigning numerical grades also means that different segments of the course need to be considered in proportion to their contribution to the whole. It is helpful to discuss the weighting of course components with other experts and professionals in the field. Students should also have the opportunity to participate in this process. Sometimes what seems inconsequential or easy to the expert educator is much more significant or difficult for the novice learner; this may provide important information in weighting course goals for grading.

Student Self-Evaluation

Although students can and should participate in the evaluation of their own learning regardless of the domain of knowledge, it is especially important that self-evaluation be used when emancipatory learning is the goal. Mezirow (1991, pp. 219-220) says it well when he argues that "dogmatic insistence that learning outcomes be specified in advance of the educational experience in terms of observable changes in behavior or 'competencies' that are used as benchmarks against which to measure learning gains will result in a reductive distortion and serve merely as a device of indoctrination." Because emancipatory learning is concerned with furthering awareness of new perspectives and achieving freedom from constraints, an instructor cannot direct or judge the learning. The student himself or herself is the only one who can describe the quality of the learning.

Using self-evaluation as a basis for course grades leads to some raised eyebrows among colleagues and objections from administrators, colleagues, or even students. Although people evaluate themselves in many other aspects of their lives, it seems that they are incapable of doing so in a classroom! Our acceptance of the teacher as sole judge and evaluator of learning is well entrenched. Because of the controversy surrounding this evaluative procedure, I review here some of the issues associated with learner self-evaluation before providing guidelines for its use.

The first reaction of many people to self-evaluation is to express the fear that students will give themselves higher ratings than a teacher would. However, there is no evidence to support this concern. In other areas, such as evaluation of teaching, the evidence indicates that, on average, self-ratings are generally lower than ratings given by others. While this may not be the case in evaluating learning, it seems most likely that some students would evaluate themselves more negatively than a teacher would, while others would evaluate themselves more positively. One cannot say which evaluation is "right," since both are interpretations of an event. The teacher has more expertise; the student is more aware of his learning. I would argue that teachers are just as likely to misjudge learning as are students.

It also should be noted that learner self-evaluations are not carried out in isolation. They should include discussion and negotiation, as should teacher evaluations. This point is discussed in the section on guidelines.

There are some circumstances in which learner self-evaluation is problematic. When students compete for grades in order to get into prestigious limited-enrollment programs or graduate studies, their desire for high grades may result in invalid self-evaluations. In this case, negotiation and validation of the evidence of learning must be carried out.

Students themselves often dislike self-evaluation. They find it difficult to do and are anxious about or embarrassed by the process. At their first exposure to self-evaluation, they may insist that this is the teacher's job and refuse to participate. As self-evaluation is not a usual practice, this reaction is hardly surprising. It is both paradoxical and foolish to force anyone to participate in an activity that is intended to be empowering. In order for students to accept self-evaluation as a viable alternative, they need to learn how to carry one out. The element of choice, however, cannot be removed. Learning how to conduct a self-evaluation becomes an emancipatory learning goal in itself. Most of us would agree that the ability to evaluate their own progress is something that students should take with them into the world of work.

Encouraging Meaningful Learner Self-Evaluation

Although Mezirow (1991) addresses evaluation of emancipatory learning only briefly and does not focus on self-evaluation, he raises several helpful points. Underlying his suggestions is the belief that such evaluation needs to focus on the quality of the reflective process rather than on specific outcomes, which cannot be delineated. Some guidelines for learner self-evaluation can be inferred from Mezirow's advice.

- Self-evaluation should focus on the amount and quality of content, process, and premise reflection.

- Evidence of greater openness to other points of view and indications of an increased awareness of the values that underlie daily life can be presented.
- Comments on the quality of participation in reflective discourse may be included in the self-evaluation.
- Students may want to describe any changes they have experienced in long-established patterns of expectations and behaviors.
- Student response to hypothetical dilemmas and reasons for their response can form a component of a self-evaluation. (Mezirow also suggests that several raters could react to the student responses.)
- Learning journals, critical incidents, or any of the strategies used to foster emancipatory learning, can contribute to its evaluation.

How does a teacher encourage meaningful student involvement in these self-evaluation strategies? First, students must examine the quality of their critical reflection and their openness to the perspectives of others; second, instructors must ensure that this is a trustworthy and credible evaluation process. Of course, there are no tried and true methods, and I still struggle daily with self-evaluation issues despite years of experience with this approach. However, some of the following suggestions may be useful.

- Students have to learn how to do self-evaluations. They often need help to clarify their goals, develop criteria for those goals, and determine what is appropriate and sufficient evidence of learning.
- Working together in pairs or small groups, learners can assist each other in clarifying goals, developing criteria, and discussing evidence.
- Instructors should discuss individually with students their self-evaluation plans to ensure they do not feel cast adrift in the process. Even though meetings are time consuming, they should occur ideally two or three times over the duration of a one-semester course.

- Students should be encouraged to evaluate their learning as they progress through the course rather than leaving it to the end. A journal or a log book can be used to facilitate this process.

- Evidence of learning can take different forms. For example, students may choose to work on projects independently, make presentations to their peers, write life stories, or conduct research in the field. To give students some guidance, particularly when self-evaluation is new to them, provide a list of suitable formats.

- Self-evaluation must include adequate validation of the evidence of learning. Just as communicative knowledge is validated through discourse and consensus (more than one person has to agree that something is a norm before it is a norm), so judgment of the quality of learning must be validated by others. Students can confirm what they have learned by presentations to the educator, their peers, professionals in the field, or any others who have expertise in the area. If feasible, more than one person should be involved.

- When learning evidence is examined by another person, the ensuing discussion must be critical and challenging, as well as supportive. The goal is to carefully weigh and interpret the evidence, clarifying what has been learned and how the evidence represents the learning.

- Final course grades should be determined during individual consultations between the learners and the educator. Students first present what they think their grades should be or perhaps suggest a range of grades if it is too difficult or uncomfortable to give a specific one. The grade must be justified by evidence of learning and validation. The educator can question the grade or ask for further clarification, but should not reject it as this defeats the purpose of the entire process. Consensus is critical here. Both students and educator must be satisfied that the grade represents the quality of the learning.

Sometimes, self-evaluation is appropriate for one component of a course, but not for the entire course. If this is the case, the guidelines given here can still be used, but rather than negotiating a final grade, the teacher and student discuss a mark for that segment of the learning.

Encouraging learner self-evaluation can be uncomfortable for the instructor as well as for students. It requires courage, respect for, and a trust in students, and the conviction that some kinds of learning can be assessed only by the learner.

Evaluating Teaching

As was discussed in Chapter One, knowledge of teaching falls primarily into the communicative domain. It includes the skills of working and communicating with others, and takes place in a social context. Teaching involves either a socialization or reformist approach. Knowledge of teaching becomes emancipatory when educators engage in critical self-reflection and thereby change their practice.

The quality of communicative and emancipatory knowledge is best judged subjectively and through self-evaluation. It is not surprising that researchers who have tried to objectify and quantify teaching behaviors and relate these to quality have not succeeded. For example, some years ago, a colleague and I analyzed many hours of videotaped teaching, noting the exact behavior that was occurring at timed intervals (Cranton and Hillgartner, 1981). We could find few statistical relationships between these counts and students' ratings of the teaching. The number of times a teacher asks questions, responds to questions, or gives examples has little to do with how well he or she does these things, and whether or not they are done in the right context, at the right time.

The most common form of instructor evaluation is ratings by students. Although this technique is often criticized (e.g., the questions are not based on thoughtful
consideration of what comprises good teaching), decades
of research has established their consistency and useful-
ness. Most colleges and universities routinely distribute
student rating forms with generally good results. However, these forms are not enough—they provide only one
tool to measure the quality of a complex set of knowledge
and skills.

In addition to rating forms, teachers can collect evidence of the quality of their work through interviewing
students, inviting colleagues to observe and report on
their teaching, accumulating unsolicited comments and
letters from students, recording assessments of student
learning, documenting their involvement in professional
development activities, or videotaping their classroom
work.

Further evaluation of teaching can be obtained from
colleagues, professional associations, administrators,
self-reports, graduates, government agencies, community
agencies, other institutions, and support services (Cranton, 1989). Each of these groups provides a different
viewpoint. For example, colleagues can review and comment on course outlines, graduates can indicate how
relevant the instruction was to their current position or
profession, and administrators can show how the educator's work contributes to the overall program. Which
kinds of information are appropriate depends on the
subject area and program.

Without a systematic approach, collecting and presenting evidence of the quality of teaching from many possible
sources can become confusing. The teaching dossier or
portfolio is now widely advocated as one means of organizing and presenting evaluations of teaching quality. In
the same way in which a photographer or a painter

presents samples of work to others, the dossier displays
materials that demonstrate the nature of a faculty member's practice. The teaching dossier was developed in the
mid-1980s when the Canadian Association of University
Teachers sponsored a project to systematize the kinds of
evidence of teaching effectiveness a faculty member
should collect. Led by Bruce Shore and his colleagues
(1986), the project identified three major areas in which
evidence can be collected (under these three headings, 49
specific items are listed).

- Products of good teaching, such as student essays and
  examination results.
- Instructor-developed materials, including course outlines, teaching innovations, and tests.
- Assessments and materials from others; for example,
  student ratings, colleague observations, and alumni
  comments.

Other ways of organizing a teaching dossier have been
proposed in the literature. Centra (1993), for example, did
a study of the use of teaching portfolios in a community
college during contract renewal decisions. His portfolio
format was comprised of three broad areas, quite different
in nature, with a total of thirteen categories.

- Motivational skills—commitment to teaching, goals orientation, integrated perception (linking classroom experience to a broader context), positive action (helping
  students achieve), and reward orientation (feeling rewarded by teaching).
- Interpersonal skills—objectivity, active listening, rapport, and empathy.
- Intellectual skills—individualized perception (seeing
  students as individuals), teaching strategies, knowledge, and innovation.

Following his study, Centra (1993) suggested that six
rather than thirteen categories would have been easier to
use. He proposed that a teaching dossier contain informa-

tion on motivational skills, goals orientation, rapport, teaching strategies, knowledge, and innovation.

Preparing a Credible and Trustworthy Teaching Dossier

Since the evaluation of teaching is subjective and based in part on self-report, it must be credible and trustworthy. Regardless of the organizational framework used, the contents of the dossier should represent an educator's work over time and from a variety of perspectives. I suggest a slightly different framework than those given above, simply because I believe it is important to include evidence of growth and development; otherwise the categories proposed by Shore and others (1986), Centra (1993), or any adaptation of them, are suitable. I recommend that evidence of the quality of teaching be collected on three dimensions of teaching:

- Documentation of what the instructor has done, including a list of courses taught, selected course outlines, samples of innovative activities or exercises, and examples of evaluation techniques.

- Evaluation of teaching from a variety of sources, including summaries of student ratings, unsolicited letters and cards from students, colleagues' reviews of course materials, or any of the other sources of information mentioned in this chapter.

- An overview of the teacher's professional development, including a statement of philosophy of practice and how it has changed over the years, a description of involvement in instructional development sessions and activities, comments on earlier evaluations of teaching and how the instructor has responded to them, samples of publications or conference presentations related to teaching, and descriptions of research on teaching.

This framework allows educators to present what they do, how others perceive it, and how they are continuing to develop their knowledge of teaching. In addition to this summary of the contents of a teaching dossier, some guidelines as to how to prepare the document may be helpful.

- Faculty should collect information for their dossiers on an on-going basis, rather than waiting until a few weeks before contract renewal comes up or a promotion application is due. Otherwise, it is too difficult to reconstruct what was done in the past. A simple system, such as a set of file folders in which to place course outlines, exemplary student essays, and letters from students works very well. The materials can be sorted and labeled for presentation.

- The dossier should contain a selection only, not every course outline developed. The list of courses taught should be comprehensive, but beyond that, educators should choose their favorite items to present. The selection should contain variety—different courses, levels of instruction, and different years—and should represent the educator's best work.

- Student ratings should be summarized in tables. Individual rating forms are almost impossible to interpret by reading through them. In fact, the negative ratings are likely to stand out much more than they do in a statistical summary.

- Examples of student responses to open-ended questions should be included verbatim. Again, it is best to include a variety, and choose especially interesting or unusual comments. The selection should not be only positive; an attempt should be made to present representative student comments. However, the section should not be lengthy—two or three pages are adequate. A short introductory paragraph can describe how the comments were chosen.

- How other evaluative information is presented depends on what that information is. A memo from a colleague describing an observation of a class or a review of course materials can be included as is. Similarly, unsolicited letters from students can be included in their original form. Permission to use such materials should be obtained.

- A statement of philosophy of practice should be short (less than one page) and clearly written. It should express the essence of what teaching means to the educator. It is especially valuable to indicate how the philosophy has evolved over time. If some of the changes in philosophy have occurred in response to earlier evaluations of teaching, mention this.
- List all participation in professional development activities, but only discuss events of special interest. If attendance at a faculty retreat on teaching, for example, was a significant event, an outline of retreat activities could be enlightening.
- The overall dossier should not be of overwhelming length. It should be attractively presented in a binder or portfolio, with a table of contents and tabs or markers to assist readers in accessing specific sections.

It takes time to prepare an interesting, easy-to-read, and credible teaching dossier. The final document should give the reader a vivid picture of who the educator is, what she or he has done, and how she or he is continuing to grow and develop as a teacher.

Summary

Evaluation of learning serves two primary purposes: to provide feedback to students so that they can improve their learning; and, to measure and communicate the quality of their learning to students themselves, administrators, employers, or interested others. The format and nature of feedback and evaluation varies with the kind of knowledge being acquired.

Although general guidelines for the provision of good feedback should be followed (e.g., feedback must be clear, detailed, frequently given, and constructive), it is equally important that the feedback given is appropriate for the nature of the learning. When learning is instrumental in nature, students need to know whether they are right or wrong, but when the learning is communicative or eman-cipatory, feedback is a balance of support and challenge.

Evaluation conducted for the purpose of reporting to others may be based on objective scores or subjective ratings. The objective format is suitable for measuring the acquisition of instrumental knowledge where there are right and wrong answers. The subjective format is appro-priate for communicative knowledge where validity is determined through negotiation and consensus. The use of either form of evaluation requires considerable care on the part of the educator. Objective tests must be clear, straightforward, and representative of the course con-tent. Subjectively rated evaluation needs to be conducted by ethical, responsible, and dedicated experts; discussion and agreement among individuals should take place dur-ing the process.

When emancipatory learning is one goal of a course or program, evaluation in the traditional sense becomes almost impossible. The traditional models impose ex-pected outcomes, a process that violates the meaning of emancipatory learning. Student self-evaluation is the way to avoid this situation. If done carefully, with stu-dents collecting evidence as to their learning and discuss-ing it with others, self-evaluation results are as trustworthy and credible as the more familiar strategies.

Knowledge about teaching is primarily communicative, and sometimes emancipatory, in nature. As such, its evaluation needs to be subjective and based on self-re-ports. The commonly used student ratings of teaching can be incorporated into a teaching dossier—a means of pre-senting a representative picture of an educator's practice to others. Teaching dossiers contain evidence of not only what we do, but also how others rate it, and how we are growing and developing as teachers.

Chapter Nine

Teaching Excellence: Case Studies

What makes for excellence in teaching? Profiles of award-winning teachers in higher education reveal that they come from a wide variety of backgrounds, have diverse philosophies of practice, and demonstrate very different teaching styles and strategies. Research tells us that people who know a lot about teaching and can adapt to differences among students are more likely to be good teachers (Shulman, 1987)—a not-too-surprising conclusion! In addition, personal values and beliefs play an important role in the development of teaching excellence (Kugel, 1993), as does participation in professional development activities (Amundsen, Greespreedt, and Moxness, 1995). Beyond these general observations, we can say very little about the characteristics of excellent teachers. I argue that this is because knowledge about teaching is largely communicative and emancipatory. There is no specific set of special technical skills that one can acquire to become a good teacher. There are no definitive rules to follow. There are no predictable outcomes to the strategies we use. Instead, we become good teachers by remaining committed to our discipline, learning more about our subject, thinking about our teaching, caring about our students, gaining experience, and continually challenging ourselves to improve.

In a sense, a paradox underlies this book. Knowledge about teaching is context-bound; it is constructed by individuals and groups through experience and dialogue. One person cannot tell another person how to teach, for that other person has his or her own personality, values, background, current situation, and philosophy. Yet, this book, and all books on teaching and learning, purport to provide the reader with knowledge about teaching. I try to avoid this contradiction by emphasizing the communicative nature of knowledge about teaching, as well as by encouraging educators to question their own beliefs and assumptions. Equally important is the questioning of the norms of the community of educators within which we work. An inquiring attitude toward our practice is more likely to lead to excellence in teaching than following any one set of guidelines. Brookfield (1990, p. 210), for example, concludes his book on becoming a skillful teacher by admonishing us, "Don't trust what you've just read. What for me are truths of skillful teaching may, for you, be partially or entirely inappropriate." He adds that his own views of teaching may well have changed by the time his book is printed and suggests the adoption of an attitude of reflective skepticism toward advice on teaching.

In this chapter, I present four case studies of teaching excellence. Each case represents a different approach to teaching and a distinct philosophy of practice. Some cases present teachers who do not use the methods I have advocated here. The case studies are chosen to reinforce the point that there is no undisputed, clear, direct path to good teaching. The cases are composites of faculty with whom I have worked, but no case represents a real person.

Jocelyn, Mathematics Professor

Jocelyn always wanted to be a university teacher, even before she fully understood what such a position involved. She loved teaching, explaining things to others, and drove her younger siblings to distraction by wanting to play school during the summer holidays. However, Jocelyn knew that she did not have the temperament for working with children—she was interested in ideas, the abstract concepts, more than people. She liked explaining things because she was interested in those things themselves. This led her to think about teaching people who were already committed to learning—grown-ups, university students.

Jocelyn enjoyed being a university student herself and did fairly well in her studies, although she was not an exceptional student. She realized that she was not creative and never would become a brilliant mathematician, but this was the subject that most appealed to her. Even though she had to struggle to grasp some concepts, she was drawn to the logical and clear beauty of mathematics. With great trepidation and concern as to whether she had the ability to keep up with the demands of the program, Jocelyn went on to graduate studies in her chosen field. After several rejections, she was finally accepted in graduate school and moved to another city to begin her work.

Jocelyn completed graduate studies without gaining any teaching experience. She chose research over teaching assistantships for financial support, and no one suggested that she should try her hand at teaching if that was her career goal. She took six years to complete graduate school, and then was ready to be a professor of mathematics.

Entering the academic world at a time when universities were growing and hiring new faculty, Jocelyn had a choice of three positions when she graduated. As a woman applicant in a male-dominated field, she had an advantage—many universities were looking for role models for their female students as a way of encouraging them to enter and stay in mathematics programs.

Jocelyn describes her first year as a professor as probably the worst year of her life. She had three different courses to teach; senior colleagues suggested that she should begin producing publications immediately; and she was expected to be the women's representative on nearly every committee in the department. But it was the teaching she faced every day that dominated her nightmares. Jocelyn's childhood dream of explaining interesting theoretical points to a rapt audience of students did not resemble the reality she faced. The students were not interested, they did not listen carefully, they did not learn, they did not understand, and they did not care that they did not learn. Her lectures were muddled and incomprehensible, even to herself as she gave them. She prepared for hours each night, but when she was in the classroom, it never turned out as she envisioned it. Some days she finished a 50-minute lecture in 15 minutes and then struggled through the rest of the class in agony. Attendance at her classes fell. Students read newspapers in the back of the room, then questioned her closely about the mid-term examination. Jocelyn only hoped that her colleagues or department chair would not find out what was happening before she figured out how to improve the situation.

She carefully avoided notices about professional development workshops or discussion groups for new faculty. She had a secret to hide, and there was no way she was going to talk about teaching to anyone until she knew what was wrong. Hiding her humiliation and embarrassment, Jocelyn determined to solve her problem herself.

Her course evaluations for that first year were mediocre, but better than she expected, and no one said anything to her about the need to improve the ratings. Through trial and error, experimentation, rehearsals held in front of the mirror late at night, and sheer hard work, Jocelyn managed to get her lectures organized so that they fit the time slots of the classes. She developed a plan for each class, and underneath that plan on the lectern was another back-up plan in case her timing was dreadfully wrong. As she walked through the halls, she noticed other teachers using overhead projectors on which were displayed outlines of the lecture. Jocelyn went to an empty classroom and learned how to operate the projector so that she could use this way of organizing her talks. She forgot about her dreams of rapt audiences, or even interested ones, but got her students to come to class by daily references to the content of the final examination. By her fourth year, as she was getting ready to apply for tenure, Jocelyn finally felt comfortable as a teacher. She did not see herself as an especially great teacher, but her classes were clearly organized, her lectures were well delivered, and she used extensive examples to illustrate the theorems she presented. About three-quarters of the students attended on any one day, there were no complaints, and student ratings were above the mid-point of the scale. After the horrors of her initiation into teaching, this seemed quite a satisfactory state.

Twenty years later, Jocelyn is the recipient of an award for teaching excellence. She carries out research on teaching mathematics, particularly strategies for encouraging young women in the field. She is often invited to speak at other universities on teaching mathematics. In these talks, Jocelyn likes to joke about her first years as a teacher. She still sees herself as a mathematician first, and a teacher second. She has never been particularly interested in instructional development activities, and resists participating in a mentor program to assist new faculty with their teaching.

In terms of psychological type, Jocelyn has preferences for sensing and thinking, and is probably more introverted than extraverted. This profile is demonstrated by her interest in content over process and subject over students. Perhaps reliance on her thinking function led Jocelyn to treat her early teaching experience as a problem to be solved, and her introversion may have inhibited her from asking for help.

Jocelyn is clear about her philosophy of teaching. She sees herself as an expert, one who is able to explain her subject to others and direct them through the intricacies of mathematics. She challenges students to do their best, sets high standards, and expects students to work hard to meet those standards. She sees critical thinking as an integral part of learning mathematics. When a student is not suited to mathematics as a field of study, Jocelyn does not hesitate to say so. She does not teach service courses, where students who are majoring in accounting or computer science take a mathematics course as a part of their requirements. The discipline comes first for her. Jocelyn rejects innovative methods, such as teamwork, and does not believe that student self-direction will work in her field. However, she is open to the use of technology in the classroom and has become quite interested in a distance education project in which her department is involved.

Jocelyn transmits instrumental knowledge and does it well. "I am a professor," she says, "therefore, I profess." Her approach to teaching would not be appropriate in some disciplines, nor would it work for all her colleagues in her own department, but it is effective for Jocelyn. Her goals are to convey knowledge, challenge students to go beyond what they think they can do, and promote purposeful problem solving and critical thinking.

Tim, English and Communications Professor

Tim's dream was to be an actor. His parents took him to plays and operas when he was a child; throughout adolescence, he was at the movie theater as often as his weekly allowance would permit. In high school, Tim joined the Drama Club and competed for roles in every play. Several times, he was chosen for lead roles—his teachers encouraged him to go on to take drama in university, and his parents were supportive. Tim was on his way to being an actor, undaunted by those sour souls who reminded him that most actors could not support themselves.

Tim's enthusiasm for drama remained unabated throughout his undergraduate years. He studied English literature, poetry, and music, but drama continued to be his central interest. He was actively involved in the university theater group and was selected to act in at least one play each term. Tim developed a strong sense of camaraderie with his theater group. Late nights of rehearsing, playing backgammon, and drinking endless cups of black coffee together led to the formation of an exceptionally cohesive group.

When Tim graduated, he moved east where there were more opportunities for acting roles and began to look for work. After six frustrating months and the humiliation of having to ask his parents for further financial help, Tim noticed an advertisement for a part-time position teaching drama at a college. This could be the answer, a way to tide himself over until he was chosen for a role. Tim's charisma and enthusiasm for drama won him the position in spite of his lack of teaching experience. The hiring committee wanted someone young and vibrant, a person who could attract students to the program.

Tim liked teaching. He did not really view his job as teaching in the traditional sense—he saw himself more as the director of a play. Important ideas came up naturally as the class read and discussed plays. Tim encouraged impromptu acting out of scenes and participated fully in this activity. He even wore costumes to class, delighting the students with his spontaneity, flamboyance, and obvious love of the theater.

Some of Tim's older colleagues found his approach to teaching frivolous and worried that he was not taking his position seriously enough. Unbeknownst to Tim, it was suggested that he not be rehired for the next term. However, when student evaluations came in, with spirited comments written on the backs of the forms, and when the registration for the next term's class was full, Tim was asked if he could teach two classes in the winter session.

Today, Tim is a full-time instructor in the Department of English and Communications, which also includes drama courses. He has started a Drama Club at the college, and although he still tries out for the occasional acting role, he sees himself primarily as a teacher. Tim's practice is not without conflict. He has frequent arguments with both colleagues and administrators at the college about his style of teaching and violation of many of the unspoken rules of conduct in the department. For example, he often invites students to his home for social gatherings and continues to dress in a manner that some view as improper for a college teacher. Generally, though, his students' enthusiasm for his courses, the high evaluations he receives, and his obvious dedication to his students override any complaints about Tim's style. Since Tim has set his sights on becoming a very good teacher, he has enroled as a part-time student in a Master of Education program.

Tim's psychological type profile shows preferences for extraverted intuition and extraverted thinking. Tim's interest in drama, his zeal for trying new things, and his indifference to the norms of the institution demonstrate his intuition. He uses his extraverted thinking to organize and plan his classes on a daily basis, as well as the overall path of his career. Deciding to return to school himself in order to learn more about teaching fits in with his preference for thinking.

Tim is articulate when it comes to talking about his teaching. He enjoys debating teaching and learning issues with his friends and colleagues. His practice has the goal of increasing students' understanding of the world around them. "Through drama," he says, "We can come to know the human condition; we can experience and therefore comprehend not only our own culture, but the culture of others." Tim sees teaching as a way of making a mark on the world, a means of changing the narrow parameters within which people live. He strongly believes that teachers should do whatever is needed to do this and reach their students, even if it means wearing costumes in class or throwing parties. He believes that it is the role of the teacher to touch the lives of students in a meaningful way, to bring something to the students they will never forget. He will go to any lengths to achieve this, and indeed his students do not forget him. Tim always has time for the many former students who drop in to say hello and tell him about the path their life has taken since they took his course.

Tim primarily facilitates communicative knowledge. His subject is one that involves mutual understanding among people through the use of language, and he treats it in an interpretive fashion. His teaching goals also include relating to students and enhancing their understanding of themselves and others. At times, Tim's teaching goals encompass emancipatory learning, especially when he encourages students to break out of their restrictive views of the world, but most of what he says and does falls into the communicative domain.

Beryl, Life Skills Professor

Beryl grew up in a poor rural community where no one was expected to go beyond high school, and many did not complete it. When Beryl was an adolescent, most boys worked on the farm and girls married young, raising their own families in the same community. Beryl was popular and happy; she liked her friends and neighbors. She married as soon as she and her boyfriend left school and within a few years had three children.

When Beryl was in her early 30s and her children were approaching their teens, their heavily mortgaged farm went bankrupt under the pressures of increasing interest rates and high costs. They moved to the city, her husband found work in a machine shop, and Beryl decided to go back to college so that she could help support their family. Being a student again was both terrifying and exhilarating, but Beryl was quick to make friends and soon was part of a group of other women reentering college. By the end of their first year, Beryl and her friends had established a support group for mature women coming back to school.

The following year, the support group caught the attention of some of the teachers in the Life Skills Program at the college. The difficulties encountered by women reentering college had never been adequately addressed and often surfaced in the life skills courses. Self-esteem, self-confidence, the changing role of women in their families, how to present oneself to the shrinking job market—these were all issues and questions that were especially important to reentering women. The faculty invited Beryl and her group to participate in the Life Skills Program as assistants. They were to receive credit for an elective practicum for their work.

This was Beryl's first taste of teaching, and she knew within a week that she had found the job she wanted to do for the rest of her life. She had empathy for the people in the course, she understood how they felt, and she knew that she could help them to deal with the seemingly insurmountable problems they faced. Beryl had been there—poverty, young marriage, children too soon, lack of education, bankruptcy—she could better relate to their lives, she thought, than middle-class teachers, however well-intentioned and pleasant they were.

By the time Beryl finished her studies, she had been working part time in the Life Skills Program for two years and was the first to apply for a one-year, full-time term contract teaching position. Everyone in the program knew the quality of Beryl's work with students, and although there was strong competition, Beryl was selected for the position.

Being a full-time college instructor turned out to be much more difficult than working as a part-time person in the program. Beryl found herself with many new and almost incomprehensible tasks. Serving on college committees, helping to write proposals for government funding for the program, approaching industry to seek further financial support, and dealing with the endless stream of memos and documents that appeared in her mailbox every day were responsibilities that Beryl had not encountered before. She struggled to balance the time required for these activities with the time she wanted to devote to her teaching.

Teaching full time, too, was far more demanding than part-time teaching. She seemed to have so many students. Beryl was used to giving students as much time with her as they wanted, but to continue to do this meant spending long hours at the college. At first, Beryl could not even keep the names of her students straight, which deeply disturbed her. The first semester was especially difficult. Beryl still loved her work in the classroom, but was pulled in so many directions that she felt she was not doing her best for the students. She agonized over this, and discussed the problem with several colleagues. Some of them told her that she was trying to do too much, that she would have to establish shorter office hours for individual meetings with students and leave it at that. Others sympathized with her reaction to full-time work and assured Beryl that she would establish a smoother rhythm with time. Everyone was kind and supportive; Beryl was certain that she could find a way to manage.

Now, Beryl has been teaching in the program for five years and has never lost the initial joy she experienced when she realized she had found her career. She puts in long hours at the college, meets individually with students daily, gives students her home telephone number and encourages them to contact her when they need to talk, and often provides that extra bit of assistance that makes the difference—helping someone to find day-care service, reviewing a résumé, or hunting up a second-hand computer. In Beryl's teaching dossier are numerous cards and letters from students expressing their appreciation of the kindness of their teacher. Beryl's marriage was not strong enough to adjust to the transformation in her lifestyle; Beryl is now divorced, but on good terms with her former husband.

Beryl's psychological type profile shows that she has a dominant extraverted feeling function and a secondary preference for extraverted intuition. It is her feeling function that leads her to care deeply for her students and help each individual in any way she can. Beryl genuinely values each learner as a human being. A preference for intuition means that a person can envision how things could be—see the possibilities in every situation. Beryl is dedicated to helping her students realize their potential. There are no limits, in her mind, as to what her students can do.

Beryl speaks passionately about her philosophy of teaching. Her primary teaching goal is to help her students overcome the problems and limitations that hold them back. Many of her students have chaotic personal lives, financial problems, and marital difficulties, but they have taken the step of returning to school. Beryl believes that she is responsible for helping them in any way she can. "I'll help a student fix up her hair and choose clothes; I'll drive someone's kids to the baby-sitter," Beryl says. "There's no limit to my job as a teacher. Life skills include all the strategies for living." Beryl finds her work profoundly rewarding. "When they make it, then it's worth every late night, every moment I've spent," she says.

Beryl fosters emancipatory learning in her students. The learners themselves have taken the initial step to change their lives, but through their work with their teacher, their perspectives change and their lives are transformed. A course on life skills includes substantial communicative knowledge as well. Students learn about the social expectations and norms of the world of work, and often the standards of a different sub-culture from the one they know. Included are such diverse topics as how to prepare a résumé, present oneself in a interview, get along in groups, and draft a personal budget. The program also focuses on personal change—self-confidence, assertiveness, communications skills. When a teacher approaches a life skills course in the way that Beryl does, these topics become the stimulus to effect dramatic and meaningful transitions in lifestyle. When students learn about alternative ways of being in the world, they then have the choice to change. This is what Beryl finds to be the deeply rewarding aspect of her practice.

André, Psychology Professor

André had no idea as a child, or even as an adolescent, of the career he would choose. He read the brochures the high school guidance counselor gave him in great detail, and he enjoyed attending Careers Day, but this did not help him make up his mind. André enjoyed sports, adventure, and such pastimes as orienteering, but he knew he could not build a career on these interests. Since he enjoyed collecting rocks, his parents suggested he consider geology, but the years of studying science did not appeal to André. He finally entered university in a general arts degree program, hoping to find something that interested him among the available courses. In the first two years of university, André spent more time going to parties, skiing, and playing bridge than worrying about a career. He was popular and had a large circle of friends. "I'm young," he would say, "I'm going to live life to the full."

In his third year of university, André began to worry about his mediocre grade point average, pressure from his parents to decide what he was going to do with his life, and his own indecisiveness. At the same time, he was taking a psychology course that appealed to him—he liked the idea that human behavior could be categorized, counted, and predicted. He was also attracted by the possibility that psychologists could help people feel better about themselves. Although he did not exactly believe he had found a calling, André could see himself helping children with behavior problems or perhaps juvenile delinquents. He told his parents he intended to be a psychologist and met with a program counselor to map out the courses needed to pursue this career. It was a relief to have everything settled.

André became involved in teaching accidentally. One of his professors asked him if he would fill in as a seminar leader in a first-year course for someone who had unexpectedly dropped out. André agreed to do this as a favor; he did not need the money and had no real interest in the job. But to his surprise, he enjoyed the experience tremendously. He liked working with the first-year students who were so full of energy and enthusiasm. He could relate well to them and did not mind if they joked around. André was popular as a seminar leader and the students' ratings were high, so when André asked if he could hold the position again in the next term, his professor agreed.

André went on to graduate studies and a university career in much the same way that he wandered into teaching. He did not consciously plan his path; rather, he took advantage of experiences as they arose, and when he found it an agreeable thing to do, he went on with it. André continued to be popular and well liked. When he applied himself to his studies, he did very well, but was never driven to be a top achiever. He always preferred a good dinner with friends to an evening with a psychology text. Indeed, he reasoned, whatever he did could be applied in some way to his understanding of human behavior.

André's first year of teaching at the university level took place before he had finished his graduate studies. The chance came up for him to take a one-year contract to replace a faculty member on a disability leave. André did not feel the pressure of being a new faculty member as the position was a temporary one. In his view it was simply excellent experience. As was the case when he was a seminar leader and a teaching assistant, André treated his teaching in a casual manner. He enjoyed the students, he was interested in the subject area, and he could just as easily talk to the class as he could listen to their discussion. The atmosphere in his classrooms was relaxed and jovial, yet the content of the courses was not neglected—André was a stickler for ensuring that all of the topics were covered and no detail left out. He did this in such an easy fashion that students never felt anxious or pushed to work faster or harder. In fact, André's students often expressed surprise at how much they had learned in such an effortless way.

After ten years of teaching, André is now an associate professor at a small university. He has published a few articles, but mainly concentrates on his teaching. His courses are preferred above all others in the program; many of his students go on in the field of psychology, even if they took their first course with André for general interest. This year, a committee of students formed to nominate André for the Alumni Association's teaching award. André's teaching style has evolved over the years.

He now incorporates a lot of experiential learning into his courses. Students take field trips to schools, clinics, and hospitals. They conduct practical research projects as course assignments. André makes frequent use of films and videotapes in the classroom. He believes that students need to experience psychological concepts, not just read about them.

André's psychological type profile reveals that he prefers extraverted sensing as a dominant function and has extraverted feeling as an secondary function. His preference for sensing shows itself in André's original indecisiveness about his career and the way he wandered into things for the sake of the experience, without a plan. Now, in his teaching, his emphasis on learning through concrete activities and field assignments reveals his own preferences in gathering knowledge. It is André's feeling function that leads him to have easy-going and warm relationships with his students and to care about the classroom atmosphere.

André enjoys talking about his teaching and is clear as to what he values. He believes that relating to the students' lives and experiences is the most important thing he can do. "Psychology is not an abstract theory," he says. "It is the study of people, and the students are people. All of their experiences are relevant to the course." Caring about the students as people, establishing a casual and happy environment in the classroom, and setting up situations in which students can experience psychology in action are valued by André. He sees himself as having three goals, as a psychology instructor. One is to give students the information they need—the history, models and theories, and background of the discipline. The second goal is to help students use psychology to understand their own lives and the lives of others. Third, for some students, André says, the study of psychology changes their lives, puts them on a new path. He values this, but would never press students into such a change if they did not show the interest. He believes that it is also perfectly acceptable if students simply learn something and enjoy it.

The three goals of teaching that André describes indicate that he works to some extent in each of the instrumental, communicative, and emancipatory domains of knowledge. Although one could question whether or not there is instrumental knowledge in the field of psychology, André would say that there is. He presents facts, rules, and procedures in his discipline—this is what initially drew him to study it, along with the hope that he could help people. Helping students to understand their own lives and those of others seems to be André's primary goal; this is clearly facilitating communicative knowledge. He ensures that the relationship between students' personal experiences and the content of the course is clear to them. Since some of André's students do change the direction of their studies as a result of taking his courses, André also fosters emancipatory learning. However, this is not a primary motive in his practice. André does not describe himself as a reformer, change agent, or provocateur. His interest in enjoying things as they are is too strong for those roles to dominate his practice.

Teaching Excellence and Teacher Preferences

Each of the teachers described in the case studies in this chapter represents a unique way to be an excellent teacher. No doubt, ten more cases would show ten more directions that good teaching can take. Jocelyn sees herself as a subject expert who is able to explain things clearly and simultaneously challenge students to reach for high standards. Tim's enthusiasm, energy, and intense interest in using drama to increase students' social understanding cannot help but rub off on his students. Beryl's deep caring for her students drives her practice. André enjoys life and expects his students to share that value. Perhaps two broad common themes emerge in these four teaching cases: caring, including caring for the discipline, the practice of teaching, and the students; and being true to oneself, being an authentic human being rather than just a teacher in a role.

Teacher self-awareness may be one of the most significant factors involved in teacher excellence. If we understand ourselves and our preferences for how we best work with others, if we can articulate and put into practice our philosophy of teaching, and if we engage in critical reflection on our practice, I believe that teaching excellence is within our reach. Caring is also necessary to achieve outstanding results. Excellent teachers care for their discipline, their teaching, and their students.

In Figure 9.1, I propose eight teacher preferences, based on psychological type theory (Jung, [1921] 1971). In Chapter Three, these preferences are elaborated on. Of course, psychological type is only one characteristic that may be relevant to an educator's teaching preferences, but taking it into consideration can enhance self-awareness. If faculty think about who they are as people and apply that knowledge to how they work in the classroom, they can develop their own unique style—one that is authentic and works for them. The following questions regarding teacher preferences are designed to encourage this reflective process. The first two questions relate to extraverted thinking, the second pair to introverted thinking, and so on, following Figure 9.1.

- Do I enjoy lecturing, explaining, and directing a class?
- Do I like to organize and structure my teaching?
- Do I reflect on my teaching after every class?
- Do I especially enjoy teaching theory and models?

Figure 9.1: Teacher Preferences

	More Extraverted	**More Introverted**
Thinking	Directing	Reflecting
Feeling	Collaborating	Personalizing
Sensing	Experiencing	Observing
Intuition	Reforming	Envisioning

- Do I prefer that students collaborate in groups?
- Do I especially care about the sense of harmony in class?
- Do I have intense personal feelings about teaching?
- Do I prefer working closely with individual students?
- Do I enjoy real, concrete, and practical experiences?
- Do I especially like an action-filled class?
- Do I like to sit back and notice the details in class?
- Am I especially sensitive to what happens in class?
- Am I enthusiastic about education as a means of reform?
- Do I see opportunities for learning around every corner?
- Do I have inexplicable hunches about what works in class?
- Do I have a sixth sense about teaching?

Who is the Perfect Teacher?

We all have a vision in mind when we contemplate excellence in teaching, perhaps someone who combines a breadth and depth of knowledge, compassion and empathy, excellent lecturing and questioning skills, and a keen sense of humor. However, focusing on such an ideal will always leave us feeling dissatisfied or guilty as we all fall short of being a perfect teacher. But we do not need to be comedians, brilliant performers, charismatic public speakers, or clairvoyant saints.

We do not learn to teach in the way we learn to drive a car. There are no easily defined skills to acquire, and the learning has no end. While it would be marvelous if we just could attend a school or program and become an excellent teacher, this will not happen. To develop as a teacher occurs in much the same way as we grow in marriage, as parents, or throughout life. It is a lifelong process.

The four cases presented in this chapter illustrate several varied approaches and styles of excellent teaching. Jocelyn is dedicated to her subject and enjoys imparting it to students. She exemplifies a common, fairly traditional approach to teaching in higher education and is an outstanding teacher. We could criticize Jocelyn for not empowering her students or encouraging them to be self-directed, but in doing so we would miss the essence of her philosophy of teaching.

Some teachers stand out immediately because of their energy, conviction, enthusiasm, and flamboyance. Tim's case study demonstrates that approach to teaching. Tim is not without his critics either. Does he overlook the serious nature of his discipline? Does he fail to explore the deeper meaning of some of the plays he presents? Does he go too far to attract attention? We can denigrate him for what he is not, or we can respect what he does well.

A profound caring for students and a deep belief in the potential of each individual characterizes yet another style of excellent teaching. Beryl gives everything of herself in order to foster emancipatory learning in her students. Her critics could argue that she does too much, has no life of her own, even sacrificed her marriage to her work, and where is the virtue in that? But, Beryl changes the lives of students, and perhaps this is what teaching is about.

Many excellent teachers are not driven by a passion for their subject or a desire to change the world. But they are dedicated professionals who care about their students and work hard to help them learn. André's case study illustrates this philosophy of teaching. André is very different from Jocelyn, Tim, or Beryl, yet his style is just as likely to lead to striking results as is theirs.

One way of analyzing our teaching practices is to relate them to our psychological type preferences. Some teachers tend to be more directive, such as Jocelyn; others tend to be more reflective in nature. Using a collaborative approach or personalizing teaching by working with individual students and small groups are equally valid preferences. Learning through experience, as André favored, is a widely advocated style. Other teachers are more restrained and reticent, but extremely sensitive to what is going on in a group. Using one's intuition to view education as a process of reform or to envision how things ought to be leads to yet another philosophy of teaching.

Each of us needs to forget about the brilliant performer we would like to be and develop our own personal style of teaching. In this way we, too, will become excellent teachers.

References

Abrami, P. C., and D'Apolonia, S. (1990). The dimensionality of ratings and their use in personnel decisions. In M. Theall, and J. Franklin (eds.), *Student ratings of instruction: Issues for improving practice*. New Directions for Teaching and Learning, no. 43. San Francisco: Jossey-Bass.

Amundsen, C., Gryspeerdt, D., and Moxness, K. (1993). Practice-centred inquiry: Developing more effective teaching. *Review of Higher Education, 16*, 329-353.

Amundsen, C., Gryspeerdt, D., and Moxness, K. (1995). Using current models of teaching development to design and evaluate instructional interventions. Paper presented at the annual meeting of the Canadian Society for Studies in Higher Education, Montreal, Quebec.

Atwood, M. (1976). *Selected poems*. Toronto: Oxford University Press.

Barrows, H. S., and Tamblyn, R. (1980). *Problem-based learning*. New York: Springer.

Belenky, M. F., Clinchy, B M., Goldberger, N. R., and Tarule, J. M. (1986). *Women's ways of knowing: The development of self, voice, and mind*. New York: Basic Books.

Berquist, W. (1992). *The four cultures of the academy*. San Francisco: Jossey-Bass.

Bloom, B. S. and others (1956). *Taxonomy of educational objectives I: The cognitive domain*. New York: Longmans.

Boyd, B.B. (1980). Developing case studies. *Training and Development Journal*, June, 113-117.

Boyd, R. D., and Myers, J. G. (1988). Transformative education. *International Journal of Lifelong Education*. 7(4), 261-284.

Boyer, E. (1990). *Scholarship reconsidered*. Princeton: Carnegie Foundation.

Brookfield, S. (1987). *Developing critical thinkers: Challenging adults to explore alternate ways of thinking and acting*. San Francisco: Jossey-Bass.

214

Brookfield, S. (1990). *The skillful teacher*. San Francisco: Jossey-Bass.

Brookfield, S. (1995). *Becoming a critically reflective teacher*. San Francisco: Jossey-Bass.

Brundage, D., and MacKeracher, D. (1980). *Adult learning principles and their application to program planning*. Toronto: Ontario Institute for Studies in Education.

Bruneau, B. (1995). Academic freedom, licence & PIs. *CAUT Bulletin, 42*, 3.

Bullough, R. V., and Goldstein, S. L. (1984). Technical curriculum form and American elementary-school art education. *Journal of Curriculum Studies, 16*(2), 14-154.

Candy, P. (1991). *Self-direction for lifelong learning*. San Francisco: Jossey-Bass.

Carr, W., and Kemmis, S. (1986). *Becoming critical—Education, knowledge and action research*. Philadelphia: Falmer Press.

CAUT Bulletin (1995). Universities will lose competitive edge. Ottawa, Ontario: Canadian Association of University Teachers, *42*(10), 1.

Centra, J. (1993). *Reflective faculty evaluation: Enhancing teaching and determining faculty effectiveness*. San Francisco: Jossey-Bass.

Chaplin, J. P. (1985). *Dictionary of psychology* (2nd ed.). New York: Dell Publishing.

Cranton, P. (1989). *Planning instruction for adult learners*. Toronto: Wall & Emerson.

Cranton, P. (1992). *Working with adult learners*. Toronto: Wall & Emerson.

Cranton, P. (1994a). Self-directed and transformative instructional development, *Journal of Higher Education, 65* (6), 726-744.

Cranton, P. (1994b). *Understanding and promoting transformative learning: A guide for educators of adults*. San Francisco: Jossey-Bass.

Cranton, P. (1996a). *Professional development as transformative learning*. San Francisco: Jossey-Bass.

Cranton, P. (1996b). Types of groups. In S. Imel (ed.). *Learning in groups: Exploring fundamental principles, new uses, and emerging opportunities*, New Directions in Adult and Continuing Education, no. 71. San Francisco: Jossey-Bass.

Cranton, P.A. and Hillgartner, W. (1981). The relationship between student ratings and instructor behaviour: Implications for improving teaching. *Canadian Journal of Higher Education, 11*, 73-81.

Cranton, P. and Knoop, R. (1994). *Psychological types and teaching styles.* Victoria, B.C.: Psychological Type Press.

Cranton, P., and Knoop, R. (1995). Assessing psychological type: The PET Type Check. *General, Social, and Genetic Psychological Monographs, 121*(2), 247-274.

Cranton, P., and Smith, R. (1986). A new look at the effect of course characteristics on student ratings of instruction. *American Educational Research Journal, 23*, 117-128.

Cross, K. P. (1990). Classroom research: Helping professors learn more about teaching and learning. In P. Seldin and Associates (eds.), *How administrators can improve teaching: Moving from talk to action in higher education.* San Francisco: Jossey-Bass.

Dawkins, J. S. (1988). *Higher education: A policy statement.* Canberra, Australia: Australian Government Printing Service.

Dewey, J. (1938). *Experience and education.* New York: Collier Books.

Deshler, D. (1990). Metaphor analysis: Exorcising social ghosts. In J. Mezirow and Associates (eds.). *Fostering critical reflection in adulthood.* San Francisco: Jossey-Bass.

Dunkin, M. J., and Precians, R. P. (1992). Award-winning university teachers' concepts of teaching. *Higher Education, 24*, 483-502.

Dunn, R., and Dunn, K. (1977). How to diagnose learning styles. *Instructor, 87*, 123-144.

Eggins, H. (1997, in press). The impact of government policy on university faculty. In P. Cranton (ed.). *National differences and universal themes in teaching and learning.* New Directions for Teaching and Learning, no. 72. San Francisco: *Jossey-Bass.*

Farquharson, A. (1995). *Teaching in practice.* San Francisco: Jossey-Bass.

Flanagan, J. (1954). The critical incident technique. *Psychological Bulletin, 51*, 132-136.

Gaff, J. (1994). Faculty development: The new frontier. *Liberal Education, 80*(4), 16-21.

216

Gagné, R. M. (1977). *The conditions of learning.* (3rd ed.). New York: Harper & Row.

Gilbert, S. (1995). Quality education: Does class size matter? *Research File, 1*(1), Association of Universities and Colleges of Canada, 1-7.

Giroux, H. A. (1991). Modernism, postmodernism, and feminism: Rethinking the boundaries of educational discourse. In H. A. Giroux (ed.), *Postmodernism, feminism, and cultural politics.* Albany, NY: State University of New York Press.

Grabove, V. (1994). Instructional support for student-directed learning in an Ontario community college. Paper presented at the Annual Meeting of the Canadian Society for the Study of Higher Education, Calgary, Alberta.

Guglielmino, L. M. (1977). Development of the Self-Directed Learning Readiness Scale. Unpublished doctoral dissertation, University of Georgia, *Dissertation Abstracts International, 38*(11A), 6467.

Habermas, J. (1971). *Knowledge and human interests.* Boston: Beacon Press.

Heimlich, J. E., and Norland, E. (1994). *Teaching style in adult education.* San Francisco: Jossey-Bass.

Held, D. (1980). *Introduction to critical theory: Horkheimer to Habermas.* Berkley: University of California Press.

Heimlich, J. E., and Norland, E. (1994). *Developing teaching style in adult education.* San Francisco: Jossey-Bass.

Herbeson, E. (1992). Personality type and self-directed learning. *The Canadian School Executive, 12,* 8-15.

Hoffman, M. (1987). Critical theory and the inter-paradigm debate. *Journal of International Studies, 16*(2), 231-249.

Imel, S. (1991). *Collaborative learning in adult education.* (ERIC Digest No. 113). Columbus, OH: ERIC Clearinghouse on Adult, Career, and Vocational Education.

Jarvis, P. (1987). *Adult learning in the social context.* London: Croom Helm.

Jackson, L., and Caffarella, R. S. (eds). *Experiential learning: A new approach.* New Directions for Adult and Continuing Education, no. 62. San Francisco: Jossey-Bass.

Jarvis, P. (1992). *Paradoxes of learning: On becoming an individual in society.* San Francisco: Jossey-Bass.

Johnston, S. (1996). Addressing the big picture: Teacher preparation as part of induction into academic life and work. Paper presented at the International Consortium for Educational Development, Finland.

Jones, G. (1994). The idea of a Canadian university. Paper presented at the conference on "The Canadian University in the Twenty-first Century," Winnipeg, Manitoba.

Jung, C. (1971, Originally published in 1921). *Psychological Types*. Princeton, N.J.: Princeton University Press.

Kincheloe, J. (1991). *Teachers as researchers: Qualitative inquiry as a path to empowerment*. London: Falmer Press.

King, P. M., and Kitchener, K. S. (1994). *Developing reflective judgment*. San Francisco: Jossey-Bass.

Kitchener, K., and King, P. (1990). The reflective judgment model: Transforming assumptions about knowing. In J. Mezirow and Associates (eds.), *Fostering critical reflection in adulthood: A guide to transformative and emancipatory learning*. San Francisco: Jossey-Bass.

Knapper, C. K., and Cropley, A. J. (1991). *Lifelong learning and higher education* (2nd ed.). London: Kogan Page.

Knowles, M. S. (1975). *Self-directed learning*. Chicago: Follett.

Knowles, M. S. (1980). *The modern practice of adult education: From pedagogy to andragogy*. Chicago: Follett.

Knox, A. (1986). *Helping adults learn*. San Francisco: Jossey-Bass.

Kolb, D. A. (1984). *Experiential learning: Experience as a source of learning and development*. Englewood Cliffs, N.J.: Prentice Hall.

Krathwohl, D., and others (1964). *A taxonomy of educational objectives II: The affective domain*. New York: McKay.

Kugel, P. (1993). How professors develop as teachers. *Studies in Higher Education, 18*(3), 315-328.

Lee, P., and Caffarella, R. S. (1994). Methods and techniques for engaging learners in experiential learning activities. In Jackson, L., and Caffarella, R. S. (eds). *Experiential learning: A new approach*. New Directions for Adult and Continuing Education, no. 62. San Francisco: Jossey-Bass.

Leslie, L. L., and Brinkman, P. T. (1988). *The economic value of higher education*. New York: ACE/Macmillan.

Loevinger, J. (1976). *Ego development: Conceptions and theories*. San Francisco: Jossey-Bass.

MacKeracher, D. (1996). *Making sense of adult learning.*
Toronto: Culture Concepts.

Maclure, S. (1988). *Education re-formed.* Sevenoaks, Kent, UK:
Hodder & Stoughton.

Marsh, H. W. (1987). Students' evaluation of university
teaching: Research findings, methodological issues, and
directions for future research. *International Journal of
Educational Research, 11,* 253-388.

McCormick, D. W. (1990). The painful emotions of prior
experiential learning assessment. *Adult Learning, 2*(2), 26-28.

Mezirow, J. (1981). A critical theory of adult learning and
education. *Adult Education, 32*(1), 3-24.

Mezirow, J. (1991). *Transformative dimensions of adult
learning.* San Francisco: Jossey-Bass.

Myers, I. G. (1985). *Gifts Differing.* (7th ed.) Palo Alto, CA:
Consulting Psychologists Press.

Mulllins, G. P., and Cannon, R. A. (1991). A teaching portfolio
for departments. *Research and Development in Higher
Education, 16,* 63-84.

Murray, H. G., Rushton, P. J., and Paunonen, S. V. (1990).
Teacher personality traits and student instructional ratings
in six types of university courses. *Journal of Educational
Psychology, 82,* 250-261.

Oddi, L. F. (1984). Development of an instrument to measure
self-directed continuous learning. Unpublished doctoral
dissertation, Northern Illinois University. *Dissertation
Abstracts International, 46*(01A), 49.

Ontario Confederation of University Faculty Associations
(OCUFA) (1994). *Sustaining scholarship: A submission to the
Ontario Council on University Affairs.* Toronto.

Patton, M. Q. (1990). *Qualitative evaluation and research
methods* (2nd ed.). Newbury Park, CA: Sage Publications.

Paul, R. W. (1990). *Critical thinking: What every person needs to
survive in a rapidly changing world.* Rohnert Park, CA:
Center for Critical Thinking and Moral Critique, Sonoma
State University.

Paulsen and Feldman (1995). Toward a reconceptualization of
scholarship. *Journal of Higher Education, 66*(6), 615-640.

Perry, W. (1970). *Forms of intellectual and ethical development
in the college years: A scheme.* New York: Holt, Rinehart and
Winston.

Pilling-Cormick, J. (1996). Development of the SDL Perception Scale. Unpublished doctoral dissertation, Ontario Institute for Studies in Education.

Progoff, I. (1983). *Life-study: Experiencing creative lives by the intensive journal method.* New York: Dialogue House Library.

Rehner, J. (1994). *Practical strategies for critical thinking.* Boston: Houghton Mifflin.

Renner, P. F. (1983). *The instructor's survival kit.* (2nd ed.) Vancouver: Training Associates Ltd.

Rice, R. E. (1991). The new American scholar: Scholarship and the purposes of the university. *Metropolitan Universities, 1,* 7-18.

Rogers, P. (1992). Transforming mathematics pedagogy. *On Teaching and Learning, 4,* 78-98.

Russell, C. (1993). *Academic freedom.* London: Routledge.

Saddy, G. (1996). Do computers change how we think? *Equinox, 87,* 54-67.

Shore, B. M., and others. (1986). *The teaching dossier: A guide to its preparation and use.* (Revised edition) Montreal: Canadian Association of University Teachers.

Shulman, L. S. (1987). Knowledge and teaching: Foundations of the new reform. *Harvard Educational Review, 57(2),* 41-14.

Simpson, E. J. (1966). The classification of educational objectives: Psychomotor domain. University of Illinois Research Project No. OE 5, 85-104.

Skolnik, M. L. (1995). Upsetting the balance: The debate on proposals for radically altering the relationship between universities and government in Ontario. *Ontario Journal of Higher Education,* 4-26.

Smythe, J. (ed.) (1995). *Academic work.* Buckingham Society for Research into Higher Education: Open University Press.

Tuckman, B. (1965). Developmental sequence in small groups. *Psychological Bulletin, 63,* 384-399.

Ume, T., and Nworgu, B. G. (1997, in press). Evaluation of teaching and learning. In P. Cranton (ed.). *Natinal differences and universal themes in teaching and learning.* New Directions for Teaching and Learning, no. 72. San Francisco: Jossey-Bass.

van Halen-Faber, C. (1996). Valuing and encouraging critical reflection in pre-service teacher education. Unpublished M.Ed. Thesis, St. Catharines, ON: Brock University.

Walden, P. (1995). Journal writing: A tool for women developing as knowers. In Taylor, K. and Marienau, C. (eds.). *Learning environments for women's adult development: Bridges toward change*. New Directions for Adult and Continuing Education, no. 65. San Francisco: Jossey-Bass.

Walleri, R. C., and Seybert, J. A. (1993). Demonstrating and enhancing community college effectiveness. In T. W. Banta and Associates (eds.) *Making a difference: Outcomes of a decade of assessment in higher education*. San Francisco: Jossey-Bass.

Weston, J. (1991). *University Affairs, 32,* 10.

Woiceshyn, J. (1992). A philosophical approach to business education. *The Canadian Journal of Higher Education, XXII-2,* 73-91.

Wlodkowski, R. J. (1990). *Enhancing Adult Motivation to Learn*. San Francisco: Jossey-Bass.

Zuber-Skerritt, O. (1992). *Professional development in higher education: A theoretical framework for action research*. London: Kogan Page.

Index

A

accountability, 36-37, 42-44

Age of Enlightenment, 4, 6, 97

authenticity, 60-61

autonomy
of faculty, 36-37
personal, 165-167

auxiliary function, 52

B

Boyd, B.B., 137

brainstorming, 117

Brookfield, S., 26, 28, 30-31, 37, 62, 71, 85, 94, 99-102, 115-118, 123-124, 126, 128, 133, 138, 154, 164, 171, 192

Brundage D., and MacKeracher, D., 28

C

Canadian International Development Association (CIDA), 31

Candy, P., 164-167

Carr, W., and Kemmis, S., 8-9

Cartesian dualism, 5

case studies, individual, 191-211

case studies and role plays, 134-137

Centra, J., 186-187

class size, 33-34

closure, 94-95

collaborative learning, 129-133

collage, 162

communicative knowledge, 7-9, 15-16, 21, 121-143
and case studies, 134-137
and collaborative learning, 129-133
and discussion, 122-129
and networks, 138-140
and role plays, 134-137
and support groups, 138-141

content reflection, 19-20, 75

cooperative education, 108

critical debate, 151-153

critical incidents, 117, 156-157

critical questioning, 74-75,
151-156

critical reflection, 18-21,
74-75, 145-163

critical thinking, 114-118

cultural diversity, 29-31

curriculum development, 75-88
evaluating learning, 85-87
evaluating teaching, 87-88
preparing learning experiences, 88-95
rationale for, 76-80
selecting methods, 82-85
sequencing learning, 80-82
setting goals of, 77-80

D

debates, 117

debriefing, 113

demonstrations, 98-104

Dewey, J., 108

dialogue, 73

differentiation, 54-55

discussion, 122-129

dominant function, 52

Dunn, R., and Dunn, K., 61, 63

E

emanciaptory knowledge,
10-11, 16-17, 21, 145-168
and critical debate, 151-153
and critical incidents strategy, 156-157
and critical questioning,
151-156
and journals, 147-151
and metaphor, 160-161
and poetry, 159-160
and games, 158
and simulations, 158

evaluation
and feedback, 171-174
and the teaching dossier,
88, 185-189
methods of, 85-88
obejctive rating, 85-87,
170, 174-176
of learning, 85-87, 169-190
of teaching, 87-89, 169,
184-190
student ratings, 87
student self-evaluation, 85-
88, 179-184
subjective rating, 86-87,
170, 176-179
teaching portfolios, 88

experiential learning, 108-114
debriefing, 113
mentors, 113
networking, 114
planning for, 111-114
purposes of, 109-110
site selection, 111-112

extraversion, 49-68

F

faculty evaluation, 43

faculty, aging, 34-35

Farquharson, A., 139

feedback, 171-174

feeling, 50-55, 58-59, 63, 67-68

financial constraints in higher
education, 36-37

G

games, 158

goals, learning, 3-21
  of communicative knowl-
    edge, 7-10
  of emancipatory learning,
    10-12
  of instrumental knowl-
    edge, 4-7

goals, setting of, 77-80

group work, 129-133

H

Habermas, J., 2, 4, 6-7, 9, 13,
20, 115

Held, D., 175

higher education, changes in,
23-45
  accountability, 36-43
  aging faculty, 34-35
  business partnerships, 38-
    39
  class size, 33-34
  cultural diversity, 29-31
  decreasing resources, 40-41
  evaluation of faculty, 43
  faculty autonomy, 36-37
  financial constraints, 35-37
  goals of, 3-21
  institutional constraints,
    40-45
  job preparation, 31-33
  language diversity, 29-30
  mature students, 25-29
  professional development,
    42

Hoffman, M., 7

I

Imel, S., 130-131, 133

inferior function, 53

institutional constraints in
higher education, 40-45

instrumental knowledge, 4-6,
13-14, 20, 97-119
  and critical thinking, 114-
    118
  and demonstrations, 98-
    104
  and experiential learning,
    108-114

instrumental knowledge
(contd.)

   and lectures, 98-104

   and problem-based learning, 104-108

Internet, the, 41, 74

introversion, 49-53, 55-59,
63-68

intuitive function, 51, 59, 60,
64, 68

J

Jarvis, P., 10-11, 23-24, 30,
165-167

job preparation, 31-33

journals, 112, 147-151

judgmental functions, 50-52,
59

Jung, C., 48-58, 67

K

Kincheloe, J., 146

Knowles, M.S., 163

Knox, A., 26, 27, 29, 137

Kolb, D.A., 59, 61-64, 109, 111

L

learner profiles, 65-66

learning style preferences, 47,
61-67

learning, collaborative
   See collaborative learning

learning, communicative
   See communicative learning

learning, emancipatory
   See emancipatory learning

learning, instrumental
   See instrumental learning

learning, problem-based
   See problem-based learning

learning, self-directed
   See self-directed learning

lecturing, 98-104

Lee, P., and Caffarella, R.S.,
109-111, 114

logbooks, 112

M

mature students, 25-29

mentors, 113

metaphor, 160-161

Mezirow, J., 19, 72, 75, 122,
179, 181-182

N

networking, 114

networks, 138-140

Norland/Heimlich Teaching
Values Scale, 56

O

objective evaluation, 170,
174-176

P

partnerships with business
and industry, 38-39

perceptive functions, 51

philosophy of teaching, 71-75

poetry, 160

premise reflection, 19-20, 75

prior learning, inclusion of,
108

problem-based learning,
104-108

procedural analysis, 81

process reflection, 19-20, 75

professional development,
diminished support for, 42

psychological type theory,
48-55, 62, 65-68

R

resources, decrease in, 40-41

role plays and case studies,
134-137

Russell, C., 39

S

self-awareness, development
of, 72-73

self-directed learning, 163-167

self-evaluation, 179-184

sensing function, 51-55, 58-59,
63-68

simulations, 158

Society for Teaching and
Learning in Higher
Education, 74

subjective evaluation, 170,
176-179

support groups, 138, 140-141

T

task analysis, 80-81

teaching dossiers, 185-189

teaching methods, 82-85
    facilitative, 83
    instructor centered, 83
    reformist, 84
    student input, 85

teaching style preferences, 55-61, 207-209

teaching, philosophy of
See philosophy of teaching

teaching, preparation for, 69-96

teaching, scholarship of, 12-20, 70

thinking, 50-55, 57, 60, 62-63, 67-68

Tuckman, B., 132-133

type profiles, 52

V

Van Tilburg/Heimlich
Teaching Beliefs Scale, 56

W

Wlodkowski, R.J., 102-103